PARASHAH
EXPERIENCING THE WEEKLY TORAH PORTION

Rachel Margolis,
Joel Lurie Grishaver &
Jane Golub

ISBN 10: 1–934527–70–x

ISBN 13: 978–1–934527–70–2

Torah Aura Productions • 4423 Fruitland Avenue, Los Angeles, CA 90058
(800) BE-Torah • (800) 238-6724 • (323) 585-7312 • fax (323) 585-0327
E-MAIL <misrad@torahaura.com> • Visit the Torah Aura website at www.torahaura.com

MANUFACTURED IN CHINA

Parashat ha-Shavua Glasses

Our friends Vicky Kelman and Gail Dorph are both fond of quoting their teacher, Dr. Joseph Lukinsky, who regularly teaches that Jews are supposed to look at the world through the lenses of the Torah portion every week.

Here is the basis of that idea.

> The Torah is divided into fifty-four portions. Because of the uniqueness of the Jewish year, which adds a whole month every couple of years, the divisions are carefully arranged so that we have a fixed part of the Torah to read each week and can finish all of it in one year (or at least read a part of each portion each year).

> Each portion has many, many truths to teach, but usually we only digest them one at a time. If we only learn one great thing each year from each *parashah, Dayenu*!

> If we can take that one good idea with us all week, and test it, and use it as part of our life, then we will have really learned and incorporated its lesson into who we are.

> By wearing *Parashat ha-Shavua* glasses we are learning the whole Torah, one piece at a time.

Consider this book a collection of fifty-four sets of *Parashat ha-Shavua* eyeglasses. We hope you see a lot of interesting and wonderful things.

Rachel Margolis, Jane Golub and Joel Lurie Grishaver

TABLE OF CONTENTS

בְּרֵאשִׁית BERESHEET

make meaning darkness commanded presence sword brought bloods
punishment creation eyes
wife woman things windy sixth
flaming haunts
children
Adam helper called listened source hunted
second accepted formed
unformed kill shine
brother forever man
great garden don mark mouth people
longer giver
dust flesh
came rested hand filled green shall
mother really lifted Cain eat deep
life keeper face settled door told die Eden
tempt embarrassed
meets pain fits didn taken
food belly nice grow
hid aren best rose placed
night guard seasons away space pregnant flock ate touch
Evil rib sent left nose wildlife
tree built voice wild fell soil birth
finished rain fallen leaves took
signs bread fifth land bone seventh sound
Abel alive grew field created
fourth stars till path Later wander plants
fruit shouts ready God sea animals
kind beasts divide dressed breath holy gift
sweat earth Good Eve
dry forbidden birds going
history saw
farm Human light strength
return sewed
look
master evening sleep living appear
cursed heavens heard angry
time crawling sneakiest serpents

Overview: Genesis 1:1-6:8

We start at the very beginning—a good place to start. God creates the world in six days, and on the Seventh Day God rests. We meet Adam and Eve, who live in the Garden of Eden and eventually are expelled from it after eating from the forbidden Tree of Knowledge. Once they leave the Garden we read of Adam and Eve's children, Cain and Abel. In the first incidence of sibling rivalry Cain kills his brother Abel and infamously asks, "Am I my brother's keeper?" We then read a list of ten generations from Adam to Noah.

OUR TORAH TEXT: GENESIS 1:27

וַיִּבְרָא אֱלֹהִים אֶת־הָאָדָם בְּצַלְמוֹ
בְּצֶלֶם אֱלֹהִים בָּרָא אֹתוֹ זָכָר וּנְקֵבָה בָּרָא אֹתָם.

ויברא אלהים את האדם בצלמו
בצלם אלהים ברא אתו זכר ונקבה
ברא אתם

God created people in God's image, in the image of God—God created them—male and female—God created them.

Exploring Our Torah Text

The first mitzvah in the Torah is "Be like fruit, and multiply." It is the blessing that God gives to the first people. It teaches that families are good things. This midrash makes a connection between "being fruitful" and other responsibilities.

> When God created the first people, God led them around the Garden of Eden and said: "Look at my works! See how beautiful they are—how excellent! I created them all for your sake. See to it that you do not spoil or destroy My world. If you do, there will be no one else to repair it" (Ecclesiastes Rabbah 7:3).

1. What does "Be fruitful and multiply" mean?

2. What is the connection between "taking care of the earth" and "being created in the image of God"?

torah experience

Our Jewish texts have a lot to say about the environment. Using these resources, create a PSA (public service announcement) to deliver to your school about the environment. Be sure to include at least one Jewish text and offer at least one way others can help the environment.

Resources

When, in your war against a city, you have to besiege it a long time in order to capture it, you must not destroy its trees, wielding the ax against them. You may eat of them, but you must not cut them down. Are the trees of the field human to withdraw before you into the besieged city? Only trees that you know do not yield food may be destroyed (Deuteronomy 20:19–20).

One should be trained to not be destructive. When you bury a person, do not waste garments by burying them in the grave. It is better to give them to the poor than to cast them to worms and moths. Anyone who buries the dead in an expensive garment violates the negative mitzvah of *bal tash<u>h</u>it* (Maimonides, *Mishneh Torah*, Mourning 14:24).

Whoever breaks vessels, or tears garments, or destroys a building, or clogs up a well, or does away with food in a destructive manner violates the negative mitzvah of *bal tash<u>h</u>it* (Kiddushin 32a).

It is forbidden to destroy anything that can be useful to people (*Shul<u>h</u>an Arukh, Laws of Body and Soul*, Section 14).

Reflection Question: Having created this PSA, how will your environmental behavior change?

MITZVAH OF THE WEEK: שְׁמִירַת הַטֶּבַע *SH'MIRAT HA-TEVA*

Shmirat ha-Tevah means "guarding the environment." Even though you won't find the words *Shmirat ha-Teva* in the Bible or in the Talmud, you will find these ideas.

Shmitah (the Sabbatical year) is a biblical rule that the land must be allowed to rest every seven years. Nothing can be planted or harvested.

Tu b'Shevat (the fifteenth of the month of Shevat) is the New Year for trees. It is a day that celebrates all things that grow in the ground.

Ba'al Tashhit (do not waste or destroy) is a biblical mitzvah that begins by teaching that when you are fighting a war you cannot cut down fruit trees to try to starve you enemy. It turns into a law that says "It is wrong to waste or destroy anything that is useful." It is the biblical recycling command.

This idea comes from our Torah text.

Shmirat ha-Teva Experience

Here are twenty things you can do to help protect the world. Check the ones you and your family are already doing. Add five more things to the list. Share your five with the whole class.

☐ Recycle paper, glass, aluminum, batteries and plastic

☐ Check your carbon footprint

☐ Check that all your toilets are water savers

☐ Turn off the water while brushing your teeth

☐ Do not buy products with a lot of packaging

☐ Sweep the backyard rather than hose down

☐ Do not buy fur, coral or ivory

☐ Use energy saver bulbs

☐ Use recycled paper

☐ Know what products at the store are "green"

☐ Don't eat non-sustainable food

☐ Do not use tropical hardwoods

☐ Carpool, bicycle or walk

☐ Plant trees

☐ Compost

☐ Know when to turn off lights

☐ Cut six-pack rings; never let helium balloons go

☐ Personally clean up your neighborhood

☐ Find a non-polluting way to light a barbecue

☐ Educate yourself, educate others

Now highlight/circle two that you would like to do at home.

Reflection Question: Having looked at these changes, which do you believe that your family can really make?

Sh'mirat ha-Teva Resources

The **Jewish Farm School** is a project designed to connect Jews to the soil. **Hazon** is an ecological organization that is particularly interested in food. **Ha'reshut Le'Shmirat Ha'teva** is the Israeli organization that focuses on preserving the environment of the Land of Israel. **Teva Learning** is a North American organization particularly concerned with Jewish environmental education.

People for the Ethical Treatment of Animals (PETA)
http://www.peta.org/

Zoo Torah
http://www.zootorah.com/

Jewish Vegetarians of North America
http://www.jewishveg.com/

Association for the Prevention of Cruelty to Animals (ASPCA)
http://www.aspca.org/

Find a URL for a recycling center in your area.

נֹחַ NOAH

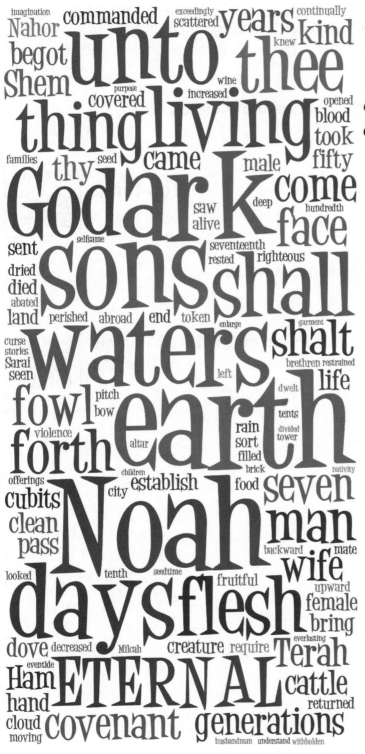

imagination commanded exceedingly years continually
Nahor scattered knew kind
begot unto thee wine
Shem purpose increased opened
covered blood
thing living took fifty
families thy seed came male
God ark come
saw deep hundredth
alive face
sent selfsame seventeenth righteous
dried rested
died sons shall
abated
land perished abroad end token enlarge garment
curse shalt
stories left brethren restrained
Sarai waters dwelt life
seen
fowl pitch bow earth tents
violence altar divided tower
forth rain sort
filled
children brick nativity
offerings establish food seven
cubits city Noah man
clean backward mate
pass tenth seedtime wife
looked fruitful
days flesh upward
female
bring
dove decreased Milcah creature require everlasting Terah
eventide ETERNAL cattle
Ham returned
hand
cloud covenant generations
moving husbandman understand withholden

Overview: Genesis 6:9–11:32

God decides the world has turned evil and must be destroyed—except for Noah, who is described as "righteous for his generation." God tells Noah to build an ark and save his family and two of every animal. After days of rain, a dove Noah sends out finds dry land. The rainbow is the symbol of the covenant God makes with Noah. When the people eventually build the Tower of Babel, God babbles their language. We are then introduced to the patriarchs with a list of generations from Noah to Abram.

OUR TORAH TEXT: GENESIS 6:9

In the Noah story, everyone is destroyed in the flood except for one person and his family. God chooses to save only Noah and those closest to him. This verse, which introduces Noah, gives us some clues about why God picked him.

אֵלֶּה תּוֹלְדֹת נֹחַ נֹחַ אִישׁ צַדִּיק
תָּמִים הָיָה בְּדֹרֹתָיו
אֶת־הָאֱלֹהִים הִתְהַלֶּךְ־נֹחַ.

אלה תולדת נח נח איש צדיק תמים
היה בדרתיו את אלהים התהלך נח

These are the stories of Noah. Noah was a righteous person for his generation. Noah walked with God.

Exploring Our Torah Text

Have your class join in this debate.

The Torah says, "Noah was righteous for his generation" (Genesis 6:9).

> Rabbi Yoḥanan said: "He was righteous for his generation but would not be considered righteous in other generations."
>
> Resh Lakish said: "If he was able to be righteous in his generation, he would have been outstandingly righteous in any other generation" (Sanhedrin 108a).

Break into two teams and debate away.

torah experience

In the Midrash and in the Talmud *(Sandhedrin 56a)* we learn that God gave Noah seven commandments that all people (not only Jews) should follow. Any person who follow these rules, which are called *Sheva Mitzvot B'nei Noah*, is considered a righteous person.

Break into small groups and brainstorm you own list of seven mitzvot that you think all people should follow.

1. _____
2. _____
3. _____
4. _____
5. _____
6. _____
7. _____

Compare your list to this actual list of the *Sheva Mitzvot B'nai Noah*.

1. Have a system of just courts.
2. Do not swear falsely with God's name; do not teach any untruths about God.
3. Do not worship idols.
4. Engage in no form of sexual assault or misconduct.
5. Do not murder.
6, Do not steal.
7. Do not cut the limb off a living animal and eat it while letting the animal live and suffer.

Explain the reason that number seven (cutting off the limb) is part of the list.

_____
_____
_____

Reflection Questions: How do rules build community?

10

MITZVAH OF THE WEEK: צַעַר בַּעֲלֵי־חַיִּים *TZA'AR BA'ALEI ḤAYYIM*

The Bible is filled with references to the animal kingdom. So are the Talmud and Midrash. Jewish thinking about animals begins with the principle that all animals are part of God's creation toward which humans bear responsibility. Animals possess sensitivity and the capacity for feeling pain. And because God is concerned with all of creation, God is very concerned that they be protected and treated with compassion and justice. Interestingly, being concerned with animal welfare can even lead to marriage, as we see in Genesis, chapter 24. When Rebecca offers to quench the thirst of the camels, Eliezer (the servant of Abraham) knows that she is destined to become Isaac's wife.

Beginning in Bible times, it is clear that not only is cruelty to animals forbidden, but mercy, kindness and compassion for them are demanded of humans by God. The rabbinic name for the offense of cruelty to animals is *tza'ar ba'alei ḥayyim* ("pain to living creatures"). People are allowed to eat meat. People are allowed to wear animal skins. But killing an animal when it is not for legitimate human need is strictly forbidden. While torturing an animal is regarded as a criminal act, caring for an animal is an act of kindness, a mitzvah of the highest order.

These laws are from the *Code of Jewish Law*, Chapter 191, Rabbi Solomon Ganzfried. This is a summary of key laws from the *Shulḥan Arukh*.

1. It is forbidden, according to the law of the Torah, to inflict pain upon any living creature. On the contrary, it is our duty to relieve the pain of any creature. However, if they cause trouble, or if they are needed for medicinal purposes or for any other human need, it is even permissible to kill them. Therefore, it is permitted to pluck feathers from a living goose with which to write, if no other pen is available. However, people abstain from doing it because of cruelty.

2. When horses drawing a cart come to a rough road or to a steep hill and it is hard for them to draw the cart without help, it is our duty to help them, because of the precept not to be cruel to animals. We do this to prevent the owner killing them in the process of trying to force them to draw more than their strength permits.

3. It is forbidden to tie the legs of a beast or of a bird in a such manner as to case them pain.

Tza'ar Ba'alei Hayyim Experience

Today animal rights activists are making many demands. Some of them are supported by Jewish law; others are not. Which of the following demands do you believe are reasonable and just? Stand in a circle. When your teacher reads an item from the list below, step into the circle. The amount you step in should indicate the level to which you believe the practice is reasonable and just.

- [ ] Using makeup that does not involve animal testing.
- [ ] Protesting hospitals that use animals for medical research.
- [ ] Protesting hospitals that use animals for organ transplants.
- [ ] Confronting people who wear fur.
- [ ] Having dogs and cats spayed and neutered.
- [ ] Demanding that everyone become a vegetarian or vegan.
- [ ] Protesting the serving of veal.
- [ ] Always using plastic, not leather.
- [ ] Trying to stop all hunting and fishing.
- [ ] Saving the spotted owls.
- [ ] Boycotting countries that still kill whales.
- [ ] Refusing to dissect animals in biology class.
- [ ] Protesting zoos, rodeos, circuses and animal exhibitions.

Reflection Question: How does showing kindness to animals make you more human?

Tza'ar Ba'alei Hayyim Resources

PETA is an animal rights organization. **Zoo Torah** provides Jewish information about the treatment of animals.

 People for the Ethical Treatment of Animals (PETA)
http://www.peta.org/

Zoo Torah
http://www.zootorah.com/

 Jewish Vegetarians of North America
http://www.jewishveg.com/

Association for the Prevention of Cruelty to Animals (ASPCA)
http://www.aspca.org/

Find a URL for a provider of rescue pets in your area.

לֶךְ־לְךָ LEKH-LEKHA

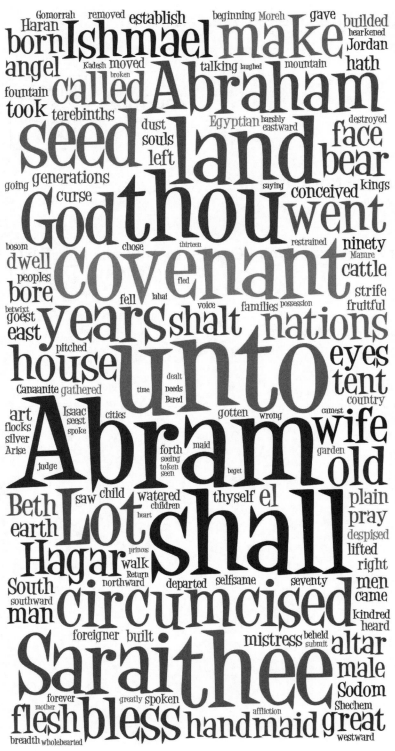

Gomorrah removed establish beginning Moreh gave builded
Haran hearkened Jordan
born Ishmael make hath
angel Kadesh moved talking laughed mountain
fountain called Abraham broken
took terebinths Egyptian harshly destroyed face
seed dust souls land eastward bear
going generations left saying conceived kings
curse God thou went ninety
Mamre
bosom chose thirteen restrained cattle
dwell covenant
peoples fled strife
bore lahai fruitful
betwixt goest years shalt families possession
east voice nations
pitched eyes
house unto tent
Canaanite gathered dealt country
time needs
Bered
art Isaac cities gotten wrong camest
flocks seest spoke wife
silver forth maid garden
Arise seeing token old
judge seen beget
saw child watered thyself el plain
Beth children heart pray
earth Lot shall despised
Hagar princes lifted
walk Return right
South northward departed selfsame seventy men
southward came
man circumcised kindred
heard
foreigner built mistress beheld altar
Sarai thee submit male
Sodom
forever greatly spoken Shechem
mother affliction
flesh bless handmaid great
breadth wholehearted westward

Overview: Genesis 12:1–13:18

"Get up and get going"—
that's what God tells
Abram in the beginning
of this *parashah*. Abram
is instructed to leave his
birthplace and his father's
home and move to Canaan.
He takes Sarai, his wife, and
Lot, his nephew, with him.
When famine strikes the
land, Abram takes Sarai to
Egypt, where they let people
believe Sarai is Abram's
sister. When they return
to Canaan Abram and Lot
go their separate ways.
God makes a covenant of
the pieces with Abram,
promising him the land
of Israel and many future
generations. Hagar, Sarai's
servant, gives birth to
Abram's first son, Ishmael.
God sets another covenant
with Abram, the sign of
which is circumcision. God
then changes Abram's and
Sarai's names to Abraham
and Sarah.

OUR TORAH TEXT: GENESIS 17:9 AND 12

In this *sidrah* Abraham receives the mitzvah of circumcision as part of the Covenant with God. This is that mitzvah:

וַיֹּאמֶר אֱלֹהִים אֶל־אַבְרָהָם וְאַתָּה אֶת־בְּרִיתִי תִשְׁמֹר אַתָּה וְזַרְעֲךָ אַחֲרֶיךָ לְדֹרֹתָם. וּבֶן־שְׁמֹנַת יָמִים יִמּוֹל לָכֶם כָּל־זָכָר לְדֹרֹתֵיכֶם יְלִיד בָּיִת.

ויאמר אלהים אל אברהם ואתה את בריתי תשמר אתה וזרעך אחריך לדרתם ובן שמנת ימים ימול כל זכר לדרתיכם יליד בית

God said to Abraham, "You should keep my covenant, you and your descendants after you, through your generations... In every generation, when a newborn boy is eight days old, you will circumcise him."

15

Exploring Our Torah Text

Brit (covenant) also is the shorthand for *Brit Milah,* which means circumcision or, more precisely, the covenant of circumcision. Healthy Jewish boys are traditionally circumcised on the eighth day after birth. Many families do a covenant ceremony for their daughters, too.

The following text from a midrash explains why God wanted circumcision as a form of covenant.

> A Roman governor named Tinus Rufus once asked Rabbi Akiva: "Whose creations are more beautiful, God's or people's?"

If you were Rabbi Akiva, how would you answer Tinus Rufus?

> Rabbi Akiva answered him, "People do the prettier work." When Tinus Rufus questioned the answer, Akiva had grain and flax brought. Then he had bread and linen brought. He said, "Is not the bread more beautiful than the grain, the linen nicer than the raw flax?"

> Tinus Rufus then asked: "If God wants circumcision, why aren't boys born already circumcised?"

> Rabbi Akiva answered him, "God gave the mitzvot to Israel as an opportunity for Israel to complete themselves" (*Tanḥumah, Tazria*).

How is *Brit Milah* like baking bread or weaving linen?

torah experience

Break into small groups:

1. What is a covenant?

   _____

   _____

2. How would your covenant with God look different today? What would you promise God? What should God promise you?

   _____

   _____

   Things God Should Promise People   Things People Should Promise God

   _____   _____

   _____   _____

   _____   _____

   _____   _____

   _____   _____

   _____   _____

   _____   _____

extra torah experience

The bar/bat mitzvah is like a renewal of the covenant at birth (*brit milah* or *brit bat*). Write a special blessing you will say at your bar/bat mitzvah to renew this covenant.

_____

_____

_____

Reflection Question: After these activities, what does covenant now mean to you?

MITZVAH OF THE WEEK—בְּרִית מִילָה *BRIT MILAH*

A *brit milah* is the sign of the covenant between God and Israel. It is a mitzvah that every male child be circumcised on the eighth day of life (health permitting). If there is a possible danger to the child, the *brit milah* must be postponed until the child is in good health. A *brit milah* is considered so important that it takes place on Shabbat, a holiday, or even Yom Kippur, if that is the eighth day.

Brit Milah Experience

The role of women has changed in Judaism in the last forty years. Women have assumed an equal role in many of Judaism's rituals and roles. Yet there is no official ceremony for welcoming baby girls into the Jewish covenant. Using the following excerpt from *The New Jewish Baby Book*, write a prayer for your own *brit bat*, a covenant ceremony for girls.

> In a number of ways, *brit milah* provides a perfect "teachable moment." Parents and grandparents have just shared the exhilarating experience of birth. The emotional high of witnessing the creation of new life, the hopes and dreams that are pinned on the new child, and the heightened awareness of relatives no longer alive to share in the experience all make the opportunity for a "teachable moment" (Michael Zeldin, *Berit Mila as Education Experience*).

My Prayer for a Brit Bat Ceremony

_____

_____

_____

_____

_____

_____

_____

_____

_____

Reflection Question:

There is a growing anti-circumcision movement in America that says that male circumcision is cruel and unnatural. Most people agree that female circumcision is really cruel. After doing these activities, what would you tell the people who are anti-male circumcision?

18

Brit Milah Resources

Healthy Children.Org lists the medical advantages of circumcision. BJE-NSW is an Australian site that explains the tradition of male circumcision (female circumcision is not a Jewish thing and can be considered abuse). The **URJ** presents a Reform point of view (rather than an Orthodox one) on circumcision. **Brit Yosef Yitzchak** is an organization (Orthodox) that helps any Jewish parent provide circumcision to his or her sons.

HealthyChildren.org
http://www.healthychildren.org

BJE NSW
http://www.bje.org.au/learning/lifecycle/britmilah.html

URJ Questions
http://urj.org/ask/questions/brit/

Brit Yosef Yitzchak
http://brityy.org

Find the URL of a Mohel (Circumciser) who works in your area.

וַיֵּרָא VA-YERA

lamb hastened worse judge things Abraham appeared Gomorrah early abide knife
sight commanded child born sweep destroy doing
wash herd turned pray terebinths
spoke laugh play spoke looked servant children
spoken afraid heare small ran Stand
earth Sodom angels
way destroy day Moriah
good saw called fine eyes heard heat
ram way angels order Isaac aside earth
lo door art men built sin wood suck house
altar hide round bear thicket sore afar sojourn circumcised deal
city offering lo Lot lifted fell blessed feast
son
nations favour didst tarry household day land
father rise sake fifty righteous conceived fetched face door
Lot righteous tree tent
righteousness turned city wife ran came tree eyes lest hand born prove
called arose wife God wash tell left pray bread age lifted
saw tent night
forgive son unleavened roof bore stay
bread heart dust laugh weaned
fifty water God men age
grew ashes women stead cakes
sake years needs came house age
hand round hastened wood Oh gave
broad urged soon

Overview: Genesis 18:1—22:24

Abraham and Sarah are generous hosts to three visitors. At the end of their visit Sarah is told that she will have a baby boy (Isaac). God plans to destroy Sodom, where Lot now lives. He tells Abraham about it. Abraham bargains with God to find just a handful of righteous people and save the city, but in the end Sodom is destroyed (and Lot rescued). Another king thinks Sarah is Abraham's sister. Isaac is born, and Sarah insists Hagar and Ishmael should be sent away. An angel later saves Hagar and Ishmael in the desert. Abraham is tested when God asks him to sacrifice Isaac.

OUR TORAH TEXT: GENESIS 18:2

One of Abraham's most important adventures happened one hot day when he was sitting in the opening of his tent. The adventure begins this way...

וַיִּשָּׂא עֵינָיו וַיַּרְא וְהִנֵּה שְׁלֹשָׁה אֲנָשִׁים
נִצָּבִים עָלָיו וַיַּרְא וַיָּרָץ לִקְרָאתָם...

וישא עיניו וירא והנה שלשה אנשים
נצבים עליו וירא וירץ לקראתם

And he (Abraham) lifted up his eyes and saw that three men were standing before him. He saw and he ran to call to them.

Exploring Our Torah Text

Here is what the Midrash does with our verse.

ABRAHAM AND SARAH'S HOSPITALITY

Abraham made it his goal in life to draw others to knowing and worshipping the one true God (Maimonides, *Guide To The Perplexed*, Part 3, 51).

For this purpose Abraham planted a beautiful orchard in Be'er Sheva. His tent was constructed with four entrances constantly open to attract guests from all directions, and every weary traveler was welcomed there with shelter and refreshments. Soon the word spread that a wonderful man had opened a free-for-all hotel in the desert.

The guests streamed in from far and near, enjoyed their meals, thanked their host, and arose to leave.

"You must say a blessing after your meal!" Abraham urged. "Say, 'Blessed be the Ruler of the Universe of Whose bounty we have eaten.'"

Sarah was equally devoted to spreading truth in the world by teaching the women. As long as Sarah was alive, the doors of the tent were always open.

Shabbat lights were never extinguished, and the food in the household was blessed with abundance (*Genesis Rabbah* 48:9, 49:7, 39:21, 60:15.).

The way the midrash describes this portion, it is directly connected to the previous story, in which Abraham was circumcised. So he is standing and running to greet visitors in the hottest part of the day.

tORAH eXPerieNce

Imagine and create a conversation between Abraham and Sarah about their need to be hospitable to these visitors.

_____

_____

_____

_____

_____

_____

_____

_____

_____

_____

_____

Reflection Question:
After creating a conversation that is missing from the Torah, what did you learn about Abraham and Sarah?

MITZVAH OF THE WEEK—הַכְנָסַת אוֹרְחִים *HAKHNASSAT ORAHIM*

Hospitality is simply making a guest welcome. And yet Judaism considers this an important mitzvah. In the Torah we learn the story of the first Jews, Abraham and Sarah. Their story is intricate and fascinating as they set out on a journey that begins the Jewish people. However, the mitzvah for which they are most known is *hakhnasat orahim*, hospitality.

In *B'reishit*/Genesis, chapter 18, Abraham has circumcised himself. According to the midrash, God visits Abraham to see how he is feeling. Abraham sees three men in the distance. Though he is still recovering, Abraham leaves God to attend to these travelers.

Rabbi Jason Miller (Hillel.org) teaches us the following.

> We learn that on the third day after Abraham had circumcised himself, he hosted three angels who appeared in human form. Recovering from this procedure in the excruciating heat of the midday sun... he ran to greet them. Not realizing these men were angels, Abraham took these strangers into his home and offered them water to wash their feet and shade to rest. With his wife Sarah's help, the guests were treated to a feast of bread and meat, curds and milk. He personally served these strangers the delicacies and attended to their needs.

What we might consider a commonplace action has now become something special, holy, a mitzvah.

Mitzvah Experience

Open up a Torah to Genesis 18: 1–8, and reread the verses about Abraham and Sarah welcoming the guests. What special things did they do? How can you make others feel welcome?

Welcome the kindergarten class for an hour of special time together. Your class can:

- play games
- read stories
- sing songs

with the kindergarteners.

Let Abraham and Sarah's actions guide you in your treatment of the younger students.

Reflection Question:
What was fun about providing *Hakhnasat Orhim*?

Hakhnassat Ora<u>h</u>im Resources

JewGether is an organization that allows Jews to travel from place to place using home hospitality provided from Jew to Jew. **Habitat for Humanity** builds homes for the homeless and the poor.

JewGether
http://www.jewgether.org/

Habitat for Humanity
http://www.habitat.org

Find a site that brings Jews together for Shabbat in your area.

חַיֵּי שָׂרָה HAUYEI SARAH

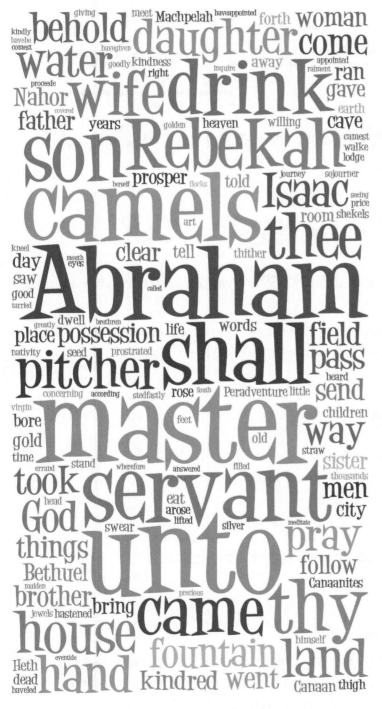

giving meet Machpelah haveappointed forth woman
kindly behold daughter come
havebe comest havegiven goodly kindness away appointed
water wife right inquire raiment ran
procede covered golden heaven willing gave earth
Nahor drink cave
father years camest walke lodge
son Rebekah
prosper flocks told journey sojourner
herself art Isaac seeing price
camels room shekels
kneel mouth thee
day clear tell thither
saw eyes
good called Abraham
tarried
greatly dwell brethren life words field
place possession shall pass
nativity seed prostrated
pitcher heard
concerning according stedfastly rose south Peradventure little send
virgin master children
bore feet old way
gold straw
time stand wherefore answered filled sister
errand thousands
took servant men
head eat arose lifted silver city
God swear meditate
things pray
Bethuel follow
maiden precious Canaanites
brother came thy
jewels hastened bring
house himself
Heth eventide hand fountain land
dead kindred went thigh
haveled Canaan

Overview: Genesis 23:1–25:18

Sarah dies (yes, ironic given the title of this *parashah*), and Abraham buys the Cave of Makhpelah for her burial place. Abraham sends a servant to find a wife for Isaac. Because Rebekkah is kind and generous, the servant picks her to be Isaac's bride. Rebekkah comforts Isaac as he mourns the loss of his mother. Abraham dies, and Isaac and Ishmael bury him in the Cave of Makhpelah.

OUR TORAH TEXT: GENESIS 23:2

At the beginning of this *parashah* Sarah dies. The Torah breaks that bad news this way.

וַתָּמָת שָׂרָה...וַיָּבֹא אַבְרָהָם לִסְפֹּד לְשָׂרָה וְלִבְכֹּתָהּ*.

ותמת שרה...ויבא אברהם לספד לשרה ולבכתה

Sarah died...and Abraham mourned her and cried.

Exploring Our Torah Text: Graphics

Why is the word וְלִבְכֹּתָהּ *v'livkotah* written with a small כ *Kaf*?

It is to teach us that Abraham did not excessively weep for Sarah because she was old and had lived a full life (Rabbi Meir Zlotowitz).

TORAH EXPERIENCE

Judaism has a number of laws and rituals surrounding death and mourning. Using the information below, split into groups and change your classroom into a *shiva* home.

Glossary

Shiva: seven-day mourning period immediately following the burial of a loved one

Minyan: ten people

Seudat ha-havra'ah: meal of condolence

kri'a: symbolic ripping of the clothing (or a black ribbon is pinned to the mourner's clothes and ripped). It symbolizes that the person who has died will always be missed, and that the mourners will not be whole again.

What happens in traditional shiva house? Reform, Reconstructionist and Conservative families may sit shiva differently.

- It is a mitzvah to make a *shiva* call
- Visitors traditionally don't exchange greetings and wait for the mourners to start a conversation.
- Sometimes visitors share these traditional words: *Ha-Makom yinakhem et-khem b'tokh sh'ar avelei Tziyon vi'Y'rushalayim* (May God comfort you among the other mourners of Zion and Jerusalem).
- Visitors should come to a *shiva* house with stories or memories of the deceased.
- Some mourners won't be interested in talking, and others will have a lot to say. Follow the cues of those in mourning.
- Often the best thing to say is nothing. Sometimes by sitting in silence you do more for a mourner than words can.
- By sharing stories of the person who has died or by joining the mourner in silence you are saying, "I am here for you. I feel your pain."
- As awkward as silence can be, it can be more effective than some misguided comments. Here are some things that seem like they would be comforting but are not appropriate to say to the mourner:

  "How are you?" (They're not so good.)

  "I know how you feel." (No, you don't. Each person feels a unique loss.)

  "At least she lived a long life." (Longer would have been better.)

  "It's good that you have other children," or "Don't worry, you'll have more." (The loss of a child, no matter what age, is completely devastating.)

  "Cheer up—in a few months you'll meet someone new." (He/she has just lost the other half of his or her soul!)

  "Let's talk about happy things." (Maybe later.)

- It is a mitzvah for visitors to bring food for the mourners.

(Adapted from **My Jewish Learning** http://www.myjewishlearning.com)

Reflection Question: Based on rehearsals (and perhaps some real experiences), what does it feel like to visit a *shiva* house?

MITZVAH OF THE WEEK: מִצְוַת מֵת MITZVAT MET

Rabbi Simlai:

The Torah begins with an act of *G'milut Hasadim* (kindness).

It also ends with an act of *G'milut Hasadim*.

It begins "And God, the Eternal, clothed them, making coats of skin for Adam and his wife," and it ends "And God buried him in the valley."

The rabbis called the mitzvah of burying someone *Mitzvat ha-Met*, the mitzvah for the dead. We might imagine that a funeral is done for the sake of the survivors, but the rabbis say, "No. A funeral is a kindness, a mitzvah, done for the deceased."

Why does the dead person need a funeral?

_____

_____

Have you ever been involved in a funeral or a shiva house? What did you do to help someone? What did someone do to help you?

_____

_____

_____

_____

Mitzvah Experience

Some laws and customs about death, burial and shiva

Study these texts with a partner. Explain their meaning to each other. Pick one text/custom that you think is most interesting in what it teaches about Jewish views of death.

1. Rabbi Ben Zion Bokser wrote: "People are mortal. They only live in the world for a while. But people are not less because they die. In some ways, it is the fact that one dies which leads one to immortality. Death is the price of life."

2. It is a mitzvah to visit all sick people without regard to race, color or creed (Maimonides, *Mishneh Torah, Laws of Mourning; Shulhan Arukh, Yoreh Deah* 335.1, 335.9).

3. A dying person should not be left alone so that he or she should not feel abandoned. Also, because a person learns something important from witnessing a death (*Shulhan Arukh, Yoreh Deah* 339.4).

4. Because the body is the place where a holy spirit lived, it should be treated with respect, even after the spirit has left. Therefore, a body is cleaned, guarded, treated with honor, and prepared for burial with respect. This is called *Kevod ha-Met*, the honor of the dead. The mitzvah of washing and preparing a body for burial is called *Mitzvat Met* (*Brakhot* 18a, *Shulḥan Arukh, Yoreh Deah* 373:5).

5. Because the act of preparing a dead body was an important, if emotionally difficult, mitzvah, Jews often organized groups called *Hevra Kadisha* (Holy Societies) (*E.J.*, 8.439).

6. It is a mitzvah to comfort mourners and to see to their needs. One goes to a funeral not only to honor the dead but to comfort the mourners (*Sotah* 14a).

Isaac Klein, *A Guide to Jewish Religious Practice*

Reflection Question: Having examined these laws and customs of mourning, what have you learned about the Jewish attitude toward death?

Mitzvat Met Resources

Here are websites of organizations that work to make facing a funeral easier for others.

The Gamliel Institute
http://www.gamliel.org/

National Association of Chevra Kadisha
http://www.nasck.org/index.htm

Kavod v'Nachum
www.jewish-funerals.org

Find a Hevra Kadisha near you.

תולדות TOLDOT

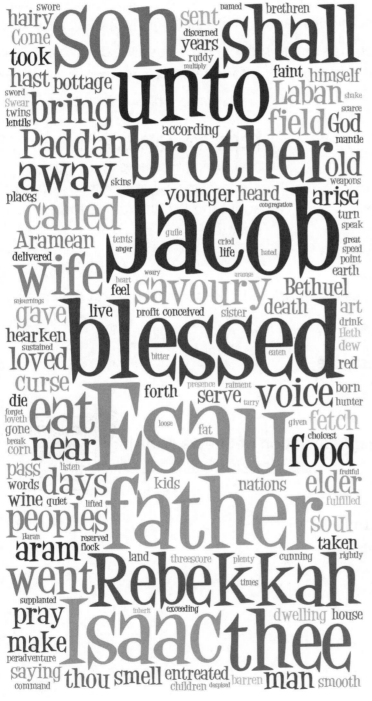

Rebekkah and Isaac are now at the center of our story. After a struggle to conceive, Rebekkah gets pregnant with twins. The twins fight inside her, and when they are born, Esau emerges first, with Jacob pulling at his heel. The brothers continue to fight, both for their parents' affection and for the birthright. One evening, after a particularly grueling day for Esau, he sells Jacob his birthright in order to get a bowl of stew. Later Isaac plans on blessing Esau. Rebekkah and Jacob trick him, and Isaac ends up blessing Jacob. In order to avoid his brother's anger, Jacob flees to Padan Aram.

OUR TORAH TEXT: GENESIS 24:67

Although this verse is found in _Hayyei Sarah_, it highlights the relationship between Isaac and Rebekkah.

וַיְבִאֶהָ יִצְחָק הָאֹהֱלָה שָׂרָה אִמּוֹ וַיִּקַּח אֶת־רִבְקָה
וַתְּהִי־לוֹ לְאִשָּׁה וַיֶּאֱהָבֶהָ וַיִּנָּחֵם יִצְחָק אַחֲרֵי אִמּוֹ.

ויבאה יצחק האהלה שרה אמו ויקח
את רבקה ותהי לו לאשה ויאהבה
וינחם יצחק אחרי אמו

Isaac then brought her into the tent of his mother Sarah, and he took Rebekkah as his wife. Isaac loved her, and thus found comfort after his mother's death.

Exploring Our Torah Text

Isaac and Rebekkah had a loving relationship. We are told about it in many places. We can find it in this story in midrash:

> Isaac then brought her into the tent of his mother Sarah _(Genesis 24:67)._ You find that as long as Sarah lived, a cloud hung over her tent (signifying the Divine Presence); when she died, that cloud disappeared; but when Rebekkah came, it retuned. As long as Sarah lived, her doors were wide open; at her death that custom ceased; but when Rebekkah came, that custom returned. As long as Sarah lived, there was a blessing on her dough, and the lamp used to burn from the evening of the Sabbath until the evening of the following Sabbath; when she died, these ceased,

but when Rebecca came, they returned. And so when he saw her following in his mother's footsteps, right away *Isaac then brought her into the tent* (Genesis Rabbah 60:16).

Rashi, the medieval commentator, explains this in a few words.

after his mother's death (Genesis 24:67). It is the way of the world: All the while that a man's mother is alive, he is attached to her, and when she dies, he is consoled through his wife (Rashi).

In the Bible we find this story:

Later, Rebecca and Isaac had trouble getting pregnant. Isaac is famous for praying on his wife's behalf.

Isaac pleaded with the Eternal on behalf of his wife, because she was barren; and the Eternal responded to his plea, and his wife Rebecca conceived (Genesis 25:21).

Questions

Based on these stories, what qualities of Rebecca and Isaac's relationship show love?

_____

_____

_____

According to this story, how would you define love?

_____

_____

_____

toraH eXperience: reality Bible

Test the relationship between Isaac and Rebekkah.
Its hardest moment is in the *sidrah*. Esau is the eldest
son. Isaac sends him out to get ready for the blessing.
Rebekkah wants Jacob to get the blessing. She plots for
him to steal it. Jacob is scared, but Rebekkah pushes
him. Jacob goes in to get the blessing. He and Isaac
talk. It is absolutely unclear (no matter how closely
you read the text) whether Isaac figures out that Jacob
is pretending to be Esau. Isaac blesses Jacob, and then
Esau shows up just after Jacob leaves. After some
begging, Isaac gives Esau a second-rate blessing.

Imagine that night. Imagine that Rebekkah and Isaac
talk about the blessing and the day's events. Write two
monologues as if a reality TV show host interviews
each of them. Then write a conversation in which they
talk to each other. Perform this conversation.

Reflection Question: What can
working with the biblical stories of
Rebekkah and Isaac teach you about
loving relationships?

MITZVAH OF THE WEEK: LOVING RELATIONSHIPS

Judaism believes strongly in loving relationships, but there is no mitzvah involved
in being in one. The closest you can come is a mitzvah in Deuteronomy 24:5
that tells a newlywed not to leave a spouse in the first year of marriage. The
problem is a filing problem. Judaism has lots of mitzvot about honesty, kindness,
love, not angering or embarrassing, etc. All of the things that might go on your
"What to do in a loving relationship" list are commanded by the Torah. Also
we have stories in the Torah, Midrash and Talmud that model being in loving
relationships. Using Rebecca and Isaac as a guidepost, along with others in your
life whom you consider to have loving relationships, create a personal reflection
on love.

Loving Relationships Experience

Create a poem, song, or picture of your own interpretations of love. Questions you might try to address could include:

- How do you share love?
- How do you want to be loved?
- What does love mean to you?
- What characteristics do you hope for in a loving relationship?

Reflection Question: How does your desire for loving relationships connect to your sense of being Jewish?

Loving Relationships Resources

Here are a number of websites that address loving relationships. See if you can find a Conservative one. We couldn't. The **Trevor Project** is an important site for gay teens, addressing (among other things) their high suicide rate.

URJ–Sacred Choices
http://urj.org/learning/teacheducate/adolescents/sacredchoices/

Chabad on Sacred Relationships
http://www.chabadtalk.com/forum/showthread.php3?t=11689

Trevor Project—It Gets Better Project
http://www.itgetsbetter.org/

Find the URL of a site where you believe that you can get good advice about relationships.

בְּרֵאשִׁ VA-YETZE

ladder ETERNAL father families
lighted Issachar
heaven blessed second tenth hearkened Simeon
speaking called stone
sheba weak awaked
days come
heard brought borne thy meet Judah
gave Jacob sheep peace
Naphtali envied near rose man reached
land Jacob sister
voice flesh tidings given wife
pillar Rachel fifth fulfilled left form gate
Rachel unto Levi
earth thy fair Leah city better
thee lifted el feast Dan
remembered hire place

bread elder ascending afraid shall poured filled
beguiled rolled Isaac came went
Beth east God tell
things eat oil sixth bore conceived service called way
sun son Gad hated Laban bone wept
saying Abraham hast raiment lie Asher month pass set
handmaid Bilhah flock men
son Leah whereon leave Luz seed
lay Dinah
house angels eyes look sleep
art abode north abide told
space awe Zilpah bearing dust
Reuben conceived west opened barren
Zebulun early south wages embraced serve
daughter bring dreamed
beautiful daughter behold judged unto
tarried
Joseph

On his way to Padan Aram, Jacob has a dream in which there is a ladder reaching from the ground to the sky. Angels are going up and coming down the ladder. God promises to be with Jacob, and Jacob awakes saying, "Surely God was in this place and I did not know it." Jacob names the place Beth El (house of God). Jacob meets Rachel at a well. He makes a deal with Laban, her father: seven years of work for Laban in exchange for marrying Rachel. After seven years Laban tricks Jacob by marrying him to Leah instead. Jacob then works another seven years to marry Rachel. Leah, Rachel and their servants (Bilhah and Zilpah) give birth to a total of eleven sons and one daughter. When Jacob and his brood leave Laban's house, Laban chases them, but they end up making peace.

35

OUR TORAH TEXT: GENESIS 28:10–11

In this *sidrah* Jacob leaves home to seek his future. On the way he has a night adventure that changes his life and that of the Jewish people. The Torah begins that story with this verse.

וַיֵּצֵא יַעֲקֹב מִבְּאֵר שֶׁבַע חָרָנָה וַיִּפְגַּע בַּמָּקוֹם
וַיָּלֶן שָׁם כִּי־בָא הַשֶּׁמֶשׁ וַיִּקַּח מֵאַבְנֵי הַמָּקוֹם
וַיָּשֶׂם מְרַאֲשֹׁתָיו וַיִּשְׁכַּב בַּמָּקוֹם הַהוּא.

ויצא יעקב באר שבע חרנה ויפגע
במקום וילן שם כי בא השמש ויקח
מאבני המקום וישם מראשתיו וישכב
במקום ההוא

Jacob went out from Beer Sheva and went toward Haran. He experienced a place and camped there for the night. Because the sun had set, he took of the stones of the place and placed them around his head, and he lay down in that place.

Exploring Our Torah Text

In the Midrash, the Rabbis ask this question:

How is prayer like the ladder that Jacob saw in his dream at Beth El?

Answer this question with a drawing.

tORAH eXPeRIeNCe

The next verse tells us that Jacob saw angels "going up" and "going down" on the ladder. This bothers the commentators a lot. They believe that angels should be first "going up" to heaven and then later "going (back) down". They spend a lot of effort to figure out why the order is reversed.

Bring a ladder into class. Divide into pairs and have each pair work out a conversation between the angels about why they went down to earth and why they are now coming back.

Perform your conversation in front of the class (on the ladder).

Reflection Question: What emerged from just a couple of words in the Torah?

MITZVAH OF THE WEEK: תְּפִלָּה TEFILLAH

It is a mitzvah for Jews to praise God by saying a hundred brakhot daily, many of these during three prescribed daily services: *Shaharit*, *Minhah* and *Ma'arev*. Even though this mitzvah is officially connected to Deuteronomy 10:20, "Be in awe, worship, hold fast, and swear by the name of The Eternal, your God," the Rabbis connected the creation of the daily services to our verse "He came to a certain place, and stopped there for the night, for the sun had set." Explaining "stopped," Rashi comments: Thus we may learn that Jacob originated the custom of evening prayer.

1. R. Jose, son of R. Ḥanina, said: "The three daily services were instituted by the Patriarchs."

    R. Joshua b. Levi says: "The three daily services were instituted to replace the daily sacrifices."

    It has been taught in accordance with R. Jose b. Ḥanina: "Abraham instituted the morning service, as it says, 'And Abraham got up early in the morning...' (Genesis 19:27); Isaac instituted the afternoon Tefillah, as it says, 'And Isaac went out to meditate in the field at eventide...' (Genesis 24:63);' Jacob instituted the evening prayer, as it says, 'And he came to the place...' (Genesis 28:11)" (*Brakhot* 26b).

37

2. Congregational prayer is always heard by God. Even if sinners are present, God does not reject public worship. One should therefore associate with congregations, and one should not pray in private when there is an opportunity to pray with the congregation (*Mishneh Torah*, Laws of Prayer, Chapter 8).

3. Prayer cannot mend a broken bridge, rebuild a ruined city or bring water to parched fields. Prayer can mend a broken heart, lift up a discouraged soul and strengthen a weakened will (*Ferdinand M. Isserman*).

Tefillah Experience

A brakhah is a way of thanking God for creating something you are experiencing. Use the formula and write three original brakhot.

Blessed are You, Eternal, our God, the One Who _____

_____

Blessed are You, Eternal, our God, the One Who _____

_____

Blessed are You, Eternal, our God, the One Who _____

_____

Reflection Question: What did you learn through writing brakhot?

Alternative Mitzvah Experience

Have your class plan and lead a school service.

Tefillin Resources

Tefillin is a set of boxes with leather straps that are used during morning weekday prayers. Tefillin comes from the same Hebrew root as *Tefillah*. Here are a number of tefillin projects that work to make them available in an affordable way. Tefillin are often associated only with men. We've included a woman's Tefillin site, too.

Partners in Torah—Tefillin Project
http://www.partnersintorah.org/programs/tefillin

Kesher Tefillin Project
http://ramahwisconsin.typepad.com/ramahwisconsin/2010/07/
kesher-tefillin-project.html

Women & Tefillin
http://www.trixrosenartphotography.com/divine-light/tefillin-
project.html

Find the best price you can for a set of Tefillin.

וישלח VA-YISHLAH

Overview: Genesis 32:4–36:43

Jacob prepares to meet Esau after many years of not seeing each other. The night before the meeting Jacob wrestles with a stranger who changes his name from Ya'akov (which referS to his pulling his brother's heel during birth) to Yisrael (one who wrestles with God). When Esau meets with Jacob in the morning they embrace and seem to let bygones be bygones. From there Jacob and his family go to Canaan, where Dinah gets involved with a man from Shekhem. On their way to Beth El Rachel dies giving birth to Jacob's twelfth son, Benjamin.

40

OUR TORAH TEXT: GENESIS 32:25-26

In this *parashah* we experience a very famous biblical wrestling match. It begins this way.

וַיִּוָּתֵר יַעֲקֹב לְבַדּוֹ וַיֵּאָבֵק אִישׁ עִמּוֹ
עַד עֲלוֹת הַשָּׁחַר. וַיַּרְא כִּי לֹא יָכֹל לוֹ
וַיִּגַּע בְּכַף־יְרֵכוֹ וַתֵּקַע כַּף־יֶרֶךְ יַעֲקֹב
בְּהֵאָבְקוֹ עִמּוֹ.

ויתר יעקב לבדו ויאבק איש עמו עד
עלות שׁחר וירא כי לא יכל לו ויגע
בכף ירכו ותקע כף ירך יעקב בהאבקו
עמו

And Jacob was left alone and he wrestled a man with him until the rising of dawn. And he saw that he could not beat him, the man struck the upper end of Jacob's thighbone as he wrestled with him.

Exploring Our Torah Text

At the end of the story in the Torah we find this verse (32:33): "Because of this, the families of Israel don't eat the *Gid ha-Nasheh* (sciatic nerve) [that is in the leg until this day]—because he tugged on Jacob's leg."

The Gid ha-Nasheh

Three talmudic commentators, Ba'alei ha-Tosafot, the Tur and Hizkuni, have a disagreement over this verse. They all ask: "Why was Israel forbidden to eat the *Gid ha-Nasheh*?" Each of them has a different answer.

Ba'alei ha-Tosafot: It is a remembrance of the great event in Jacob's life. We do it to honor him and to learn from his example.

The Tur: It is to separate one's self from danger. Jacob's children separate themselves from the thing that injured their father. It is explained by this example. It is just like a person who gets a headache each time he eats a given kind of food. He learns to give up that food.

Hizkuni: It is a punishment to remind us of the sons of Jacob who left him alone that night when he was facing danger.

Do you like one of these explanations, or do you have a better one of your own? Explain or expound!

tORAH eXPeRIeNCe

Who is the stranger? Compare your answer to these midrashic answers. Pick one.

*   Angels bring people's prayers up to heaven (*Torat Or* 1:7a).
*   The angel was Esau's guardian angel (*Genesis Rabbah* 77.3).
*   The angel was an angel named Israel who gave Jacob his name (*Hekhalot* 4.29, *Zohar* II, 4b).
*   The angel represents Rome (*Ramban ad loc*).

Meet with people who share your answer and discuss why you picked it.

Reflection Question: Do you believe in angels?

MITZVAH OF THE WEEK: אֱמוּנָה FAITH

Emunah: There is an argument about whether or not אֱמוּנָה *Emunah* (faith) is a mitzvah. Rambam (Maimonides) says that faith is demanded and lists thirteen articles of faith. Ramban (Nachmanides) says that faith cannot be commanded; all that can be commanded is acting as if one believes. Below are Maimonides' articles of faith. Circle the numbers of the ones you believe in. Put an X through the numbers of the ones you strongly disbelieve. Share your answers.

1. Belief in the existence of the Creator, Who is perfect in every manner of existence and is the Primary Cause of all that exists.

2. The belief that God is absolute and there is no Oneness like God.

3. The belief that God is not physical, nor will God be affected by any physical event.

4. The belief that God is eternal.

5. The obligation to worship God alone and no foreign false gods.

6. The belief that God communicates with people through prophecy.

7. The belief that the prophecy of Moses (the Torah) is central.

8. The belief that Torah comes from God.

9. The belief that the Torah doesn't change.

10. The belief that God is all-powerful.

11. The belief that God rewards and punishes.

12. The belief that the Messiah will come bringing a Messianic era.

13. The belief in the resurrection of the dead.

Emunah Experience

Work with a small group and make your own list of thirteen things Jews should believe today.

1. _____

2. _____

3. _____

4. _____

5. _____

6. _____

7. _____

8. _____

9. _____

10. _____

11. _____

12. _____

13. _____

Reflection Question: Is belief an important part of your Jewish connection? If not, what is?

Emunah Resources

These two organizations are the only foundations (we could find) that use Emunah in their title. They are very different. **Emunah.org** runs programs for children in Israel. **The Emunah Foundation** (probably Orthodox) works on teaching *Emunah*.

Emunah
http://www.emunah.org

The Emunah Foundation
http://www.theemunahfoundation.org

Find a Jewish foundation/NGO that uses the word "faith" in its name.

וישב VA-YE-SHEV

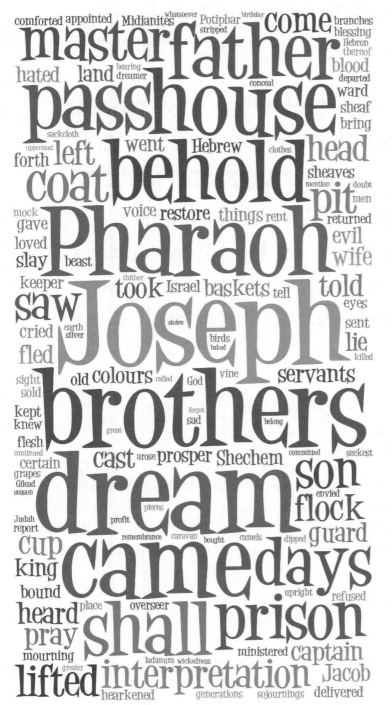

Not learning from his own upbringing, Israel (Jacob) plays favorites—and everyone knows Joseph is his favorite son. Israel makes him a coat of many colors that helps to distinguish him from his siblings. Joseph is a dreamer who shares his dreams with his family. Two such dreams involve sheaves of wheat and the sun, moon and stars bowing down to him. One day when Joseph goes to meet his brothers in the field they attack him and throw him into a pit. They steal his special coat and use it to trick Israel into thinking that Joseph was killed. Instead, his brothers sell him into slavery, and Joseph is taken to Egypt to serve in Potiphar's house. Joseph does well there, eventually becoming the lead slave. When scandal breaks, he is thrown into jail, where he interprets two prisoners' dreams.

OUR TORAH TEXT: GENESIS 37:10

In this *sidrah* Joseph has two dreams that he shares with his family.

וַיְסַפֵּר אֶל־אָבִיו וְאֶל־אֶחָיו וַיִּגְעַר־בּוֹ אָבִיו...
הֲבוֹא נָבוֹא אֲנִי וְאִמְּךָ וְאַחֶיךָ לְהִשְׁתַּחֲוֹת
לְךָ אָרְצָה.

ויספר אל אביו ואל אזיו ויגער בו
אביו הבוא נבוא אני ואמך ואזיך
להשתזוות ארצה

And he (Joseph) told (the dream) to his father and brothers, and his father scolded him... "Are we—I and your mother and your brothers—to bow down to the ground before you?"

Exploring Our Torah Text

Rashi explains this verse by saying that Jacob also said to Joseph, "Your mother Rachel is long dead. Your dreams are cruel." Rashi then explains that "Jacob was harsh with Joseph to show his other sons that he was as hard on Joseph as on any of them."

What dream is Rashi explaining? _____

_____

What did Joseph's dream do to the family? _____

_____

Torah Experience

If you were Joseph, how would you change your dream so that it would feel less cruel to your family? Work with a partner and write a dream journal for Joseph.

_____

_____

_____

_____

_____

_____

_____

_____

_____

Reflection Question: Share a dream that you have never shared before.

MITZVAH OF THE WEEK: שְׁלוֹם־בַּיִת SHALOM BAYIT

Shalom Bayit means "family peace". It is not really a mitzvah but a Jewish value that gets presented a lot in the Bible, the Talmud and the Midrash. It basically says that families should get along. It includes:

- Spouses should treat each other respectfully and kindly.
- Children should honor parents.
- Parents should respect children.
- Siblings should treat each other well.
- Grandparents and great-grandparents should be respected and honored.

In other words, everyone should get along.

Shalom Bayit Experience

Act out the following situations. Try to get to *Shalom Bayit* in each case.

Grandmother doesn't like her granddaughter's fashion choices.

Son is tired of his parents' nagging about homework and the state of his room.

Mother is angry that Father is always working.

Father is angry that his children are never ready to go to school.

Sister is angry that younger sister is always borrowing her things.

Brother wants to go out and not stay home to babysit.

Grampa is upset that Gramma is still trying to change him.

Each of two brothers thinks that their parents favor the other.

Reflection Question: What makes *shalom bayit* difficult? (Why do so many family fights happen?)

Shalom Bayit Resources

Some *Shalom Bayit* organizations stand against domestic abuse. Others are organized to stand in support of family health. Here are a couple of examples. Find out what is in your community.

 Shalom Bayit—Bay Area Jewish Women Working to End Domestic Violence
http://www.shalom-bayit.org/

Nishmat on Shalom Bayit
http://www.yoatzot.org/topic.php?id=99

 Tides—What's Possible on Shalom Bayit
http://www.tides.org/community/project-directory/show/project/single/title/shalom-bayit/

Find a site that gives advice on how to make family life easier.

מקץ MIKETZ

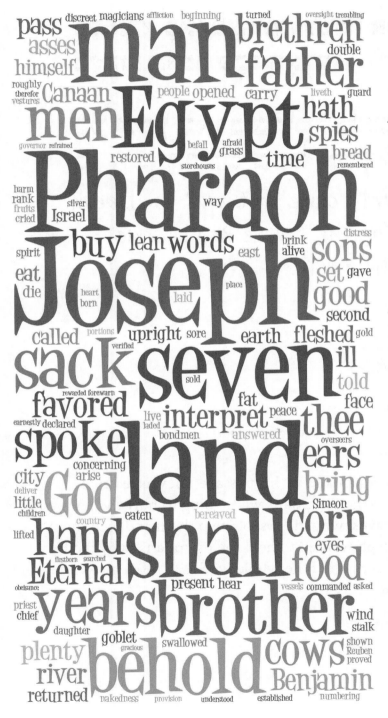

Overview:
Genesis
41:1—44:17

Joseph interprets Pharaoh's two dreams and predicts a famine. He offers practical suggestions regarding the future food shortage, so Pharaoh puts him in charge of famine control. Joseph gets married and has two sons in Egypt (Menasheh and Efraim). Joseph's prediction comes true—seven years of surplus are followed by a famine. Jacob sends ten of his sons to buy food in Egypt, keeping Benjamin safe at home. Joseph's brothers do not recognize him, but he knows who they are. Without revealing himself to them, he tricks them, returns their gold and demands they bring their youngest brother back with them. When they return with Benjamin, Joseph plants a goblet in Benjamin's bag and tells the brothers whoever has stolen the goblet will be thrown in jail.

OUR TORAH TEXT: GENESIS 41:57

This *parashah* is the one where Joseph exits jail, passes go and winds up as Pharoah's right-hand man. He sets up both a tax system and a welfare system. This verse tells us what happens.

כָּל-אָרֶץ בָּאוּ מִצְרַיְמָה לִשְׁבֹּר אֶל-יוֹסֵף
כִּי-חָזַק הָרָעָב בְּכָל-הָאָרֶץ.

כל ארץ באו מצרימה לשבר אל יוסף
כי חזק הרעב בכל ארץ

And all the earth came to Egypt to Joseph to buy food, for the famine had become strong in all the earth.

Exploring Our Text
Questions

Why did Joseph set up a system to feed non-Jews and non-Egyptians?

When the rabbis looked at this passage, they asked two questions: (1) If the Egyptians were going to hurt the Jews and make them slaves, why did Joseph help them and feed them? (2) Even if Joseph wanted to help the Egyptians, why did he set up a system that fed the whole world? *(Babylonian Talmud*, tractate *Bava Batra*, page 9b)

What is your theory?

torah experience

Why do you think Joseph set up a system to feed non–Jews and non–Egyptians?

Here is a Jewish folk story. See if it can expand our understanding.

A Banquet in Heaven

A righteous man was permitted by God to get a preview of the world to come. In a celestial palace he was ushered into a large room where he saw people seated at a banquet table laden with delicious food, but not a morsel had been touched. The righteous man gazed in wonder at the people seated at the table. They were hungry and wanted to eat—but did not!

"If they are hungry, why is it they don't eat and enjoy the food before them?" asked the righteous man.

"They cannot feed themselves," said his heavenly guide. "If you will notice, each has his arms strapped so that no matter how he tries, he cannot get the food into his mouth."

"Truly, this is hell," said the righteous one as they left the hall.

The heavenly attendant escorted him across the hall into another room, where the righteous man observed another beautiful table, equally laden with delicacies. Here, however, he noticed those seated around the table were well fed, happy and joyous. To his amazement, he saw these people also had their arms strapped.

He turned to his guide and asked: "How is it that they are so well fed even though they are unable to transport the food to their mouths?"

"Behold," said the heavenly guide. The righteous man looked on with wonder as he watched each one feeding his neighbor. The straps, he noticed, were tied to allow enough freedom for each individual to feed his neighbor, even though he was unable to feed himself.

"This is really heaven," said the righteous man.

"In truth it is," the guide answered. "As you can see, the difference between hell and heaven is a matter of cooperation."

Make a puppet show of this story.

continue with quesrions on page 52.

What is the message of this story? _____

_____

_____

How does it help you better understand Joseph's actions? _____

_____

_____

MITZVAH OF THE WEEK: מָזוֹן MAZON

While it is not on the official list of 613 individual mitzvot, this week we will focus on one aspect of *Gemilut Hasadim* called *mazon*—feeding the hungry. (It is part of some other mitzvot dealing with all kinds of caring.)

There is an American Jewish organization called **Mazon: A Jewish Response to Hunger** that feeds both the Jewish and the non–Jewish poor. On its brochure *Mazon* has a quote from the prophet Isaiah. What does it mean?

> If you offer your compassion to the hungry and you feed the famished creatures, then your light will shine in the darkness and your gloom will be like noonday (Isaiah 58:10).

What Mazon Does

Mazon asks that you contribute a suggested amount of 3% of the cost of your *simha*—a bar or bat mitzvah, a wedding, a birthday or anniversary, or any joyous occasion. Just three percent: to a cost of $1,000, add $30; to $5,000 add $150; to $10,000 add $300.

Consider being like Joseph on the day of your bat or bar mitzvah.

Mazon Experience

Now you try. Joseph created a plan that would help to feed the Egyptians. Here are some things your class can do to help feed the hungry in your area.

• Set up or join the synagogue food collection program.

• Visit a food pantry and volunteer.

• Run a sandwich-a-thon (students make sandwiches and pack healthy lunches) and donate the lunches to the homeless. If it's not in the budget, ask students to bring in the various items. Parents can volunteer to deliver sandwiches.

Mazon Resources

Mazon is a national Jewish food program. The others are regional. Find one near you.

Mazon: A Jewish Response to Hunger
http://mazon.org/

SOVA Community Food and Resource Program (Los Angeles)
http://www.jfsla.org/SOVA

Harvey Kornblum Jewish Food Pantry (St. Louis)
http://www.jfcs-stl.org/our-services/basic-needs/

The Mitzvah Food Project (Philadelphia)
http://www.jewishphilly.org/page.aspx?id=205069

Find the URL of a "feed the hungry" program in your area.

וַיִּגַּשׁ VA-YIGASH

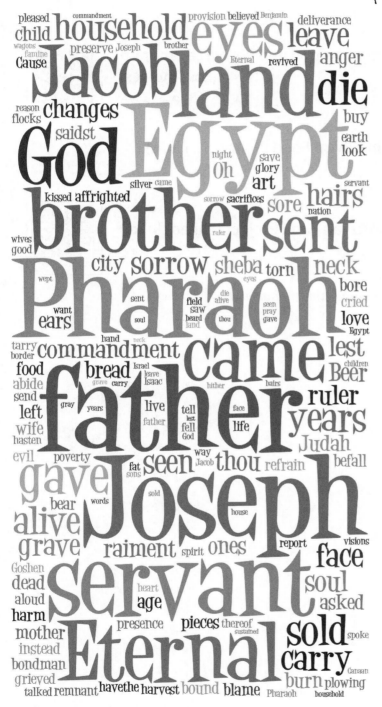

pleased commandment provision believed Benjamin deliverance
child household eyes leave
wagons preserve Joseph brother Eternal revived anger
famine Cause
Jacob land die
reason changes saidst buy
flocks God Egypt earth look
night Oh save glory
silver came art servant
kissed affrighted sorrow sacrifices sore hairs nation
brother sent ruler
wives
good
city sorrow sheba torn neck
wept sent field die alive bore
want saw seen cried
ears soul heard thou pray love
hand land gave Egypt
tarry commandment came lest
border neck
food Israel bread grave carry leave Isaac hither hairs children Beer
abide
send left gray years live tell face ruler years
wife father father lest fell life Judah
hasten God way
evil poverty seen thou refrain befall
gave fat Jacob
sons sold
bear words house
alive Joseph
grave raiment spirit ones report visions
Goshen face
dead servant soul
aloud heart asked
harm age
mother presence pieces thereof sold spoke
instead sustained
bondman Eternal carry
grieved Canaan
talked remnant havethe harvest bound blame burn plowing
Pharaoh household

Overview: Genesis 44:18–47:27

Judah pleads on behalf of his brother, Benjamin, and their father. Joseph can no longer hide his identity and reveals himself to his brothers. They are surprised, and an emotional reunion occurs. Pharaoh invites all of Joseph's family to live in Egypt. Jacob moves his family to Egypt.

OUR TORAH TEXT: GENESIS 45:4-5

We are almost at the end of the book of Genesis. In this *sidrah* comes the climax of the Joseph story. In these two verses Joseph finally reveals himself to his brothers. When he does, the outcome is a surprise. The commentaries say that Joseph is repenting here.

וַיֹּאמֶר אֲנִי יוֹסֵף אֲחִיכֶם...וְעַתָּה אַל־תֵּעָצְבוּ
וְאַל־יִחַר בְּעֵינֵיכֶם כִּי־מְכַרְתֶּם אֹתִי הֵנָּה
כִּי לְמִחְיָה שְׁלָחַנִי אֱלֹהִים לִפְנֵיכֶם.

וַיאמר אני יוסף אזיכם...ועתה אל
תעצבו ואל יזר בעיניכם כי מכרתם
אתי הנה כי למזיה שלזני אלהים
לפניכם

And Joseph said to the brothers, "I am Joseph...and now don't be sad and don't be angry that you sold me. I am here to bring life. To do that, God put me before you."

Exploring Our Torah Text

Saadia Gaon (in *The Book of Beliefs and Opinions* 5:5) taught there were four steps to achieving *t'shuvah*.

Confession: admitting you have done something wrong and stating you will never repeat the action.

Remorse: feeling bad about the hurt you have caused.

Seeking forgiveness: asking the person you have wronged to forgive you. Also, asking God to forgive you.

Accepting responsibility: finding your own way to never repeat this action.

Joseph's brothers sold him into slavery. Yet years later he was able to forgive them and welcome them into his home. How do you forgive when forgiving is hard?

With Judah's selfless offer to stay behind as a hostage in place of Benjamin, Joseph finally knew for sure that his brothers' old attitude had changed. (Abarbanel)

Does Joseph do the right thing here?

Does he meet Saadia's criteria for repentance?

torah experience

Recreate the dialogue inside Joseph's brain with one side wanting to forgive his brothers and the other side not.

Reflection Question: Describe a time when you were really conflicted.

MITZVAH OF THE WEEK: תְּשׁוּבָה T'SHUVAH

In Numbers 5:7 we are specifically told: **"They shall confess their sin that they have committed."** In that verse the mitzvah of *t'shuvah*, repentance, is rooted. However, the story of this week's Torah portion, the reconciliation of Joseph and his brothers, gives us a great opportunity to talk about forgiveness and change.

As Joseph became reconciled to his brothers from the midst of weeping, so will the Holy One redeem Israel from the midst of weeping, as it says, "They shall come with weeping, and with supplications. I will lead them; I will cause them to walk by rivers or waters" (Jeremiah 31:9) (*Genesis Rabbah* 93:8,11-12).

T'shuvah Experience

People in Twelve Step programs call it "making amends". They make a list of people they have harmed. Then they go and apologize to each person. Stage each of these apologies.

- Eve to Adam, for serving him fruit from the forbidden tree in the middle of the garden.
- Cain to Eve, for killing her son Abel.
- Abraham to Sarah, for selling her as his sister to the king of Egypt.
- Rachel to Jacob, for helping her sister and father fool Jacob into marrying the wrong woman.
- Jacob to his other eleven sons, for making Joseph his favorite.
- Jacob to Joseph for making him his favorite.
- Joseph to his brothers for telling them his self-centered dreams.
- The brothers to Joseph for selling him into slavery in Egypt.

Reflection Question: What is Jewish about an apology?

T'shuvah Resources

Beit T'Shuvah (The House of Return) is a Jewish addiction treatment center. It uses Judaism, and particularly the process of *t'shuvah* and the Twelve Steps, to help people recover from addictions.

 Beit T'shuvah
http://www.beittshuvah.org/

Find a URL that talks about the connection between t'shuvah *(repentence) and recovery.*

יְחִי VA-YEHI

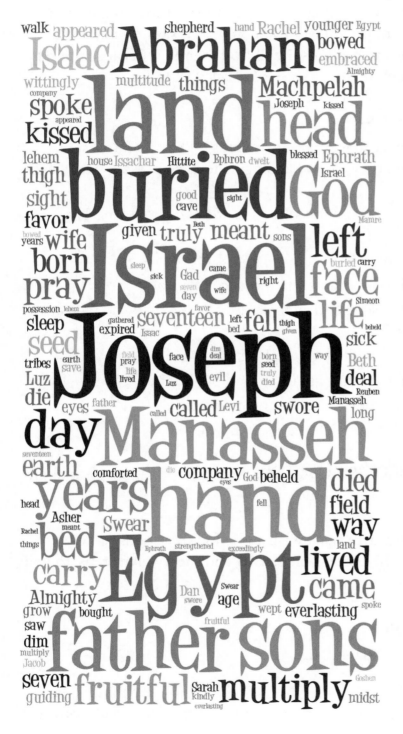

Jacob is dying, and Joseph promises to bury him in the Cave of Makhpelah in Canaan and not in Egypt. Jacob calls in Joseph's sons to bless them. Just as Jacob, the younger, received the blessing that should have gone to the firstborn, so Jacob blesses Efraim first, and then Menasheh. Jacob then blesses his own twelve sons. Joseph dies and is buried in Egypt.

OUR TORAH TEXT: GENESIS 48:20

Close to his death, Jacob blesses Joseph's sons, Efraim and Menasheh. Our verse is this famous blessing.

וַיְבָרֲכֵם בַּיּוֹם הַהוּא לֵאמֹר בְּךָ
יְבָרֵךְ יִשְׂרָאֵל לֵאמֹר יְשִׂמְךָ אֱלֹהִים
כְּאֶפְרַיִם וְכִמְנַשֶּׁה...

ויברכם ביום ההוא לאמר בך יברך
ישראל לאמר ישמך אלהים כאפרים
וכמנשה...

And he (Jacob) blessed them, saying, "Through you will Israel be blessed," as they will say, "May God make you like Efraim and Menasheh."

Exploring Our Torah Text

It is a custom for Jewish parents to bless their children at the Erev Shabbat (Friday night) dinner table. It grows from our verse. Here is the ceremony.

Blessing the Children
- Place your hands on your child's head.
- Say the appropriate blessings (sons or daughters).
- Add your own wishes and thoughts.
- Say the priestly blessing (for all children).
- Hug, kiss, etc.

For Sons

יְשִׂימְךָ אֱלֹהִים כְּאֶפְרַיִם וְכִמְנַשֶּׁה. *Y'simkha Elohim k'Efrayim v'khi-Menasheh*

May the Eternal make you like Efraim and Menasheh.

For Daughters

יְשִׂימֵךְ אֱלֹהִים כְּשָׂרָה רִבְקָה רָחֵל וְלֵאָה. *Y'simekh Elohim k'Sarah, Rivka, Rahel, v'Leah.*

May the Eternal make you like Sarah, Rebekkah, Rachel and Leah.

For All Children

יְבָרֶכְךָ יי וְיִשְׁמְרֶךָ. *Y'varekh'kha The Eternal v'yishm'rekha.*

יָאֵר יי פָּנָיו אֵלֶיךָ וִיחֻנֶּךָּ. *Ya'er The Eternal Panav elekha vi-huneka.*

יִשָּׂא יי פָּנָיו אֵלֶיךָ וְיָשֵׂם לְךָ שָׁלוֹם. *Yissa The Eternal Panav elekha v'yasem l'kha ahalom.*

May the Eternal bless and guard you. May the Eternal shine Divine light upon you and be good to you. May the Eternal face you and give you peace.

Here is a formula for your own blessing (fill in the blanks for your imagined children).

May God bless you with _____ and _____ .

May you be (like)_____ and _____ .

May this Shabbat of _____

May you be (like)_____ and _____ .

fill you with _____ and _____

torah experience

Invite the parents to join this session as a small class family day. First split the class into groups of parents and kids and ask two questions—"What are parents obligations to children" and "What are children's obligation to parents". Then report the lists and write them on the board.

Next, split the parents and kids into groups in which the generations are mixed, but the adults are with students who are *not* their children. Have these groups make a list of ways they can help each other meet expectations.

Report back to the class. If there is time, have the parents and kids meet in small family units to talk about the day.

Reflection Question:

How did working as a family change this experience?

MITZVAH OF THE WEEK: OBLIGATIONS TO CHILDREN

While blessing one's children is not a mitzvah (only a *minhag*), the Torah does list a series of obligations parents have to children. The Talmud puts it this way:

> A father is obligated to circumcise his son, redeem him, teach him Torah, take a wife for him and teach him a trade. Some authorities say to teach him to swim also (*Kiddushin 29a-30b*).

> A father must provide for his daughter clothing and covering and must also give her a dowry so that people may be anxious to woo her and so proceed to marry her. And to what extent? …Up to a tenth of his wealth (*Ketubot 52b*).

> When a father who refused to support his child was brought before Rabbi Ḥisda, he would say: "Make a public announcement and proclaim: 'The raven cares for its young, but this man does not care for his young'" (*Ketubot 48b*).

Mitzvah Experience

Imagine that you are a U.N. commission. Write a children's bill of rights.

A child shall _____ .

A child shall _____ .

A child shall _____ .

A child shall _____ .

A child shall _____ .

A child shall _____ .

A child shall _____ .

A child shall _____ .

A child shall _____ .

A child shall _____ .

Reflection Question: What would you rate as parents' big responsibilities?

Obligations to Children: Resources

In almost every Jewish community there is an organization called Jewish Family (& Childrens') Services. Here are a few examples.

 Children's Rights Inc.
http://www.childrensrights.org/

Declaration of the Rights of a Child
http://www.un.org/cyberschoolbus/humanrights/resources/
plainchild.asp

 Jewish Family Services (Los Angeles)
http://www.jfsla.org

Jewish Family Services (Detroit)
http://www.jfsdetroit.org

 Jewish Family Services (Tidewater)
http://www.jfshamptonroads.org

Find an organization in your community that tries to help children or families.

שמות SHEMOT

The second book of Torah begins with "And these are the names of the Families-of-Israel," a phrase meant to link God's promises to the ancestors we read about in Genesis to the oppression and slavery in Egypt. A new Pharaoh comes to rule who does not know the history of Jews in Egypt, and he sees the Jewish people as a threat to national security. He turns the Jewish people into slaves, and because he still fears an uprising, he orders that all Jewish boy babies be killed. Despite Pharaoh's orders, Jewish midwives Shifra and Puah save many baby boys, including Moses. He is born, hidden, found floating in a basket, raised in Pharaoh's house, turned into an outlaw when he kills to defend a Hebrew slave and is married to Tzipporah, the daughter of the High Priest of Midian. God talks to Moses from a burning bush and calls on him to lead the Jewish people to freedom.

nurse houses alive affliction midwives ETERNAL daughter children Pharaoh Moses Israel God Egypt son spoke serve Joseph enemies brick bulrushes delivered Abraham

OUR TORAH TEXT: EXODUS 2:1

In the first *sidrah* in Exodus we meet Moses. His story begins with this seemingly unremarkable sentence.

וַיֵּלֶךְ אִישׁ מִבֵּית לֵוִי וַיִּקַּח אֶת־בַּת־לֵוִי.

וילך איש מבית לוי ויקח את בת לוי

A man from the tribe of Levi married a woman from the tribe of Levi.

Exploring Our Torah Text

In Exodus 6:20 we are told that Moses' father's name was Amram, and that his mother's name was Yokheved. In our Torah text they are referred to on as "a man" and "a woman". Why do you think the Torah chose to delay the introduction of their names"?

torah experience

1. The first parashah of Shemot seems to go out of its way to say that women were crucial to Jewish survival. We meet the midwives, Moses's mother and sister, Pharaoh's daughter, and Jethro's daughter—all of whom have an important role in saving the Jewish people. In fact, no men seem to help. What lesson can you learn from this?

2. In the Midrash on Numbers we are given a clue. It says:

   In that generation the women rebuilt many of the Torah laws that men had broken. When Aaron asked everyone to give their gold jewelry to make the golden calf, the men agreed and the women refused. When the spies urged everyone to abandon the Promised Land of Israel as a destination, the men were unwilling to enter the land, but the women retained their faith in God's command.

   In other midrashim we learn that (a) after Pharaoh condemned all Jewish baby boys to death, the men wanted to abandon having children, but the women insisted on continuing; (b) women insisted on teaching their children Hebrew and giving them Hebrew names rather than adopting Egyptian culture; and (c) when most Jews abandoned infant circumcision, the women of the tribe of Levi maintained it.

How do you explain these insights? What do they teach us about the man and the woman from the tribe of Levi? How can you be like them?

Reflection Question: What can we learn from all these *midrashim* about women?

MITZVAH OF THE WEEK: שֵׁם עִבְרִי A HEBREW NAME

In the Midrash on Song of Songs (IV.12.1) we learn:

> Rabbi Huna said in the name of Bar Kappara: As a reward for four practices the Jews were redeemed from Egypt: (a) they did not change their Hebrew names, (b) they continued speaking Hebrew as their language, (c) they did not inform one on each other, and (d) they did not intermarry with the Egyptians.

Even though it is not an official mitzvah, based on this midrash we know that it is good for Jews to learn Hebrew and to have Hebrew names.

Tell everything you know about your Hebrew name. Explain how it works. What does it mean? Where does it come from?

What does your Hebrew name mean to you?

Shem Ivri Experience

You will need Hebrew naming books, Hebrew naming websites, Hebrew dictionaries, etc. In groups, pick a Hebrew name for your class. Then vote on the name as a whole class.

Reflection Question: Why are names important?

Shem Ivri Resources

There are lots of places on the net that make it easy to find a Hebrew name.

Yalla—Youth Access to Hebrew Language Literacy and Advancement
http://www.thenextbigjewishidea.com/ideas/entry/yalla-youth-access-to-hebrew-language-literacy-and-advancement

Kveller
http://www.kveller.com/pregnancy/Naming/Choosing_A_Name.shtml

Google Yourself. Who shares your name?

וָאֵרָא VA-ERA

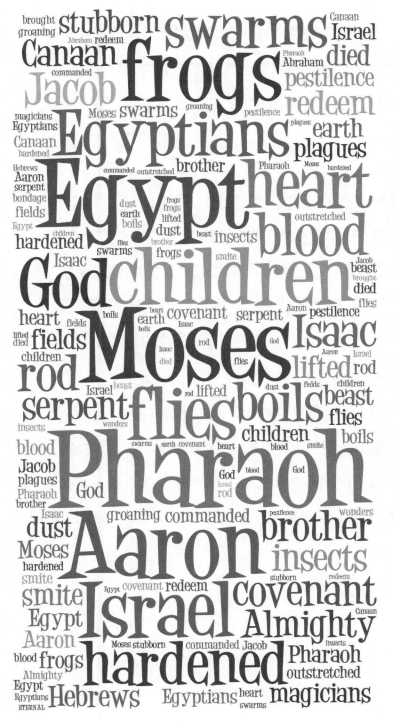

swarms frogs Egyptians Egypt heart God children Moses Isaac blood Pharaoh Aaron Israel hardened serpent flies boils rod

Overview: Exodus 6:2–9:15

Moses returns to Egypt, and his brother Aaron joins him as he talks to the people of Israel and to Pharaoh. Pharaoh doesn't believe in the power of their God, and he challenges Moses to prove God's might. Moses turns his staff into a snake that eats the snakes of Pharaoh's magicians. Moses and Aaron say to Pharaoh, "Let my people go." They visit him repeatedly with this message, and each time Pharaoh says, "No." The first seven plagues afflict Egypt for every "no" answer: blood, frogs, lice, insect swarms, cattle disease, boils and hail.

OUR TORAH TEXT: EXODUS 6:3-4

At the end of the last *sidrah* Moses and Aaron confront Pharaoh for the first time. It gets them nowhere. This *sidrah* begins with God giving Moses a pep talk, urging him to keep on struggling. Our verses are the first time God speaks in this conversation.

וָאֵרָ֗א אֶל־אַבְרָהָ֛ם אֶל־יִצְחָ֥ק וְאֶֽל־יַעֲקֹ֖ב בְּאֵ֣ל שַׁדָּ֑י
וּשְׁמִ֣י יי לֹ֥א נוֹדַ֖עְתִּי לָהֶֽם. וְגַ֨ם הֲקִמֹ֤תִי אֶת־בְּרִיתִי֙
אִתָּ֔ם לָתֵ֥ת לָהֶ֖ם אֶת־אֶ֣רֶץ כְּנָ֑עַן אֵ֣ת אֶ֧רֶץ מְגֻֽרֵיהֶ֛ם
אֲשֶׁר־גָּ֖רוּ בָֽהּ.

וארא אל אברהם אל יצחק ואל
יעקב באל שדי ושמי יי לא נודעתי
להם וגם הקמתי את בריתי אתם לתת
להם את ארץ כנען את ארץ מגריהם
אשר גרו בה

"And I appeared to Abraham, to Isaac, to Jacob as *El Shaddai*, but the four-lettered name "the Eternal" was not known to them. And also I established my covenant with them, to give them the Land of Canaan, the Land in which they lived."

Exploring Our Text

In our Torah text we learn that God makes a formal gift to the Jewish people of the Land of Canaan. Here is the question: Just because God gave it to us, is it a mitzvah to live there? Here ais a *t'shuvah* (legal "Dear Abby"–style question) sent to a famous Jewish legal scholar. It asks about the obligation to live in Israel. Write your own answer. You'll find the scholar's answers on the next page.

THE QUESTION:
T'shuvot Rabbeinu Nissim Gerondi, no. 38

> Reuven, Shimon and Levi joined together in a plan to cross the Mediterranean Sea to be closer to Eretz Yisrael. They made the following agreement, which they signed under solemn oath: Before us, the undersigned witnesses, and before Rabbi Yosef of Marseilles and Rabbi Chaim Tzarfati, they agreed to sail in October or November on a vessel from the port of Barcelona, Spain, bound for that destination, for the purpose of settling in *Eretz Yisrael* or near it, in Cyprus or Alexandria, Egypt. Now Shimon wants to recant his vow because his wife refuses to go along with him. Her relatives convinced her not to follow her husband and to refuse to accept a *get* from him. Besides, he surmises that she is pregnant. He says that if he had known that she would not join him, he would not have sworn to emigrate. He is asking whether his vows can be annulled and, if so, whether he needs Reuven's and Levi's consent, since they swore to go together.

Work out your answer to this case.

torah experience

THE ANSWERS
T'shuvot. Rabbeinu Nissim Gerona no. 38

Study the answer.

> This is indeed a severe oath, one that you should avoid like a snake...But a man is not permitted to leave his wife, and he cannot demand that she follow him to the ends of the world....I agree that this vow should be annulled. As for the question whether the consent of Reuven and Levi is needed...in this case, if Shimon received no consideration of favor from Reuven and Levi to induce him to make the vow, it may be annulled in their presence, even without their consent. But if he did receive a consideration or favor from them and because of it he made the vow, then he must do his utmost to obtain Reuven's and Levi's agreement to the annulment. However, if they are unwilling to give their consent, the vow may be annulled in any event, for the reason set forth.

Now create a piece of art that shows your connection to the Land of Israel.

MITZVAH OF THE WEEK: עֲלִיָּה לְאֶרֶץ יִשְׂרָאֵל LIVING IN THE LAND OF ISRAEL

When you read the Ramban (Rabbi Moshe ben Nahman, who is not the Rambam), he points you directly to Numbers 33:53:

> You shall take possession of the Land (of Israel) and settle it, for I have given the Land to you to possess it.

The Ramban reads this verse and says: "Living in the Land of Israel is a mitzvah"—and he seems to be right.

Here is the problem: When you look into Maimonides' list of mitzvot, *aliyah* is not there. When you read *Sefer ha-Hinukh,* another famous list of mitzvot, *aliyah* is also missing. When you dig deep into the Talmud, you can find a lot of statements that say living in *Eretz Yisrael* is good, desirable, meritorious and probably better for Jews—but it is hard (except for Nahmanides, the Ramban) to find a legal source that says Jews have an obligation to move to Israel (before the Messiah comes).

Experiencing Aliyah

Based on your opinion, which of these should be Jewish obligations regarding Eretz Yisrael?

☐ Every Jew should include Israel in his or her prayers.

☐ Every Jew should study the Land of Israel.

☐ Every Jew should financially support the State of Israel.

☐ Every Jew should politically support the State of Israel.

☐ Every Jew should visit the Land of Israel at least once in his or her life.

☐ Every Jew should spend at least one year studying in and/or volunteering in the Land of Israel.

☐ Every Jew should seriously consider moving to the Land of Israel.

☐ Every Jew should move to the Land of Israel.

Reflection Question: Play "Jeopardy". Try to recreate the questions these responsa are answering.

Aliyah Experience II: Nefesh b'Nefesh (http://www.nbn.org.il/index.php)

Write five questions about making *aliyah* (moving) to Israel. Use this website to answer your questions.

1. _____

2. _____

3. _____

4. _____

5. _____

Reflection Question: What are your thoughts about getting to Israel?

Aliyah resources

Here are some other websites to help you understand the process of making *aliyah*.

The Jewish Agency
http://www.jafi.org.il/JewishAgency/English/Home/

Gov.il
http://www.gov.il/FirstGov/TopNavEng/EngSituations/
ESNewImmigrantsGuide/

Making Aliyah Blogspot
http://movingtonahariya.blogspot.com/

Find a blog that talk about making *aliyah*.

בא BO

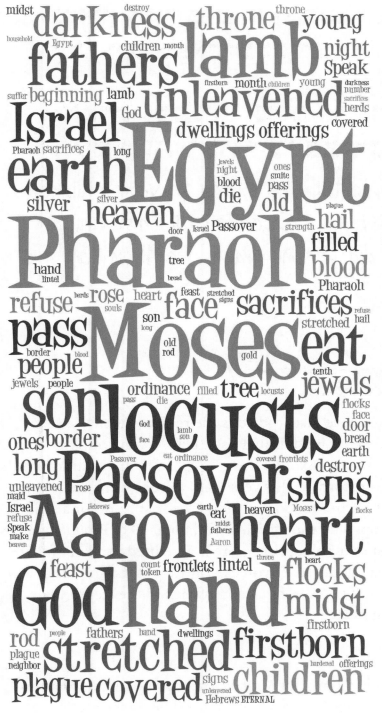

Overview:
Exodus
10:1—13:16

Moses and Aaron continue to approach Pharaoh about freeing the people of Israel, and he keeps saying no. The plagues continue: locusts, darkness and finally the death of the firstborn. God teaches the mitzvah of the new month along with a detailed explanation of the festival of *matzah*, instructions on the paschal offering in Egypt and placing blood on the doorposts—our first Passover! The exodus begins.

73

OUR TORAH TEXT: EXODUS 13:8

The first Passover took place in Egypt before the Exodus ever happened. It took place on the last night in Egypt, the night of the death of firstborn sons. Our verse comes from the directions for that seder.

וְהִגַּדְתָּ לְבִנְךָ בַּיּוֹם הַהוּא לֵאמֹר בַּעֲבוּר זֶה
עָשָׂה יי לִי בְּצֵאתִי מִמִּצְרָיִם.

וְהִגַּדְתָּ לְבָנֶיךָ בַּיּוֹם הַהוּא לֵאמֹר
בַּעֲבוּר זֶה עָשָׂה יי לִי בְּצֵאתִי מִמִּצְרָיִם

And you should tell the story to your children on this day, saying, "Because of that which the Eternal did for me when I went out of Egypt."

Exploring Our Torah Text

The verse we have just studied is the reason we have a seder each year. A seder is a family lesson plan, a way for parents to tell the story of the Exodus from Egypt to their children. The ones who transformed this verse into a seder were the rabbis of the *Mishnah*. In that book we find the first rules for a seder. When you open up the *Mishnah* to chapter 10 of *Pesahim* you find the first seder blueprint. Here is an edited version of that passage. Read it and see if you can figure out the steps that are involved. See if you can figure out which of the steps in our seder are missing.

Mishnah Pesahim 10

On *Erev Pesah*, from after *Minhah* one may not eat until after dark. Even a poor Jew may not eat until he or she reclines at the seder. Even a poor Jew—a person who lives off tzedakah—must not drink less than four cups.

When the first cup is filled, one says the *Kiddush*. *Beit Shammai* and *Beit Hillel* differ over the order of the two *Kiddush* brakhot.

One then brings vegetables. The green is dipped before the breaking of the loaf. Then they bring *matzah*, greens, h̲aroset, and two cooked dishes. In the days when the Temple existed the bones of the *Pesah̲* offering were also brought.

Then the second cup is poured. Next the child asks the four questions. If the child doesn't have enough understanding, the parents must provide instruction. According to the child's knowledge, so is the teaching done. The parent begins with the story of our shame and ends with the story of God's glory. The parent starts the explanation with the words "My ancestor was a wandering Aramean" (Deuteronomy 26:5) and then works through the entire portion.

Rabban Gamaliel taught that every seder must include a discussion of *pesah̲*, *matzah*, and *maror*. Then one says the beginning of the *Hallel*.

Beit Shammai and *Beit Hillel* disagree on how much of the *Hallel* is said before the meal. Then comes a concluding brakhah about redemption. Rabbi Tarphon and Rabbi Akiva disagree about the text of this brakhah.

Then the third cup is poured and *Birkat ha-Mazon* (the Grace After Meals) is said, followed by the rest of the *Hallel*.

When you open a modern Haggadah you find a list of fifteen steps in our seder. Put the parts of the seder in order. The best way of doing this is using a deck of 3" x 5" or 5" x 7" cards, ordering and reordering them.

_____ Four Questions	_____ Salt Water and Parsley	_____ Door for Elijah
_____ *Urh̲atz* (Washing)	_____ Eat *Matzah*	_____ Light Candles
_____ Second Cup	_____ Eat Horseradish	_____ *Dayeinu*
_____ Third Cup	_____ Hunt for *Afikoman*	_____ *H̲ad Gadya*
_____ Fourth Cup	_____ Chicken Soup with *Matzah* Ball	_____ *L'shanah ha-Ba'ah b'Yerushalayim*

torah experience

Here is Rabbi Nachman of Bratzlav's explanation of the seder.

> God, so to speak, is camouflaged in stories. These are the stories of Creation and of Adam and Eve, the stories of the Flood and of the Patriarchs and Matriarchs, the stories of Jewish exile and redemption. God is hidden in all the stories of human history. And in the as yet untold stories of each and every human being: his trials, her tribulations, and their salvation.
>
> At the *Pesah* seder we tell stories—*maggid*. We recount the stories of the Exile in, and the redemption from, Egypt. These represent the collective stories of humankind. They typify the individual stories of each and every one of us. As we retell the details of these stories, we must relate to them. See the Hand of God in the stories of our own lives.
>
> Through the telling, we bring to life their stories. In turn, may God bring to life the story of our Redemption *(Likutey Halakhot, Nedarim 5:6-8)*.
>
> And when the *Mashiah* comes, he will also tell stories. Of what we all have been through every day of our lives. The meaning of our past suffering, the redeeming effect of our past tribulations *(Rabbi Nachman's Stories #10, The Burger and the Pauper, p. 229)*.

Tell the story of the Exodus in the first person. Find places in your own life that fit into the story of the Exodus.

Reflection Question: How is the story of the Exodus your story?

MITZVAH OF THE WEEK: וְהִגַּדְתָּ לְבִנְךָ TELL YOUR CHILDREN

It is a mitzvah on the eve of the fifteenth of Nissan to tell your child the story of the Exodus from Egypt. We hold a Passover seder as a formal way of doing this telling. Rather than a seder being a temple service, it is intentionally held in the home so that each family will have their own way of telling each of their own children. The Talmud makes it very clear that each child must be told this story in the way that will make it most real and most significant for her or him. A seder is a family affair.

List three special things your family does at your seder. How does each enhance the holiday?

Experiencing Higgid'ta l'Vanekha

The whole experience of the seder is supposed to be told in the first person. Have your class tell the story of the Exodus by completing these sentences.

1. When I was a slave in Egypt my job was…

2. When I was a slave in Egypt the one thing I knew about the Land of Israel was…

3. When Moses came to Egypt and promised to take us out, I…

4. When I was in Egypt the worst of the plagues was…

5. When I left Egypt and it was my first night in the wilderness, I…

6. My best friend in Egypt was…

7. When we left Egypt, my best friend was…

8. When I left Egypt, I took…

Reflection Question: In what ways are you still a slave? What things hold you in slavery?

Higgid'ta L'vanekha Resources

Unfortunately there is still a lot of slavery and there are a lot of captives in the world today. Remembering that we were slaves gives us a big obligation to help others who are still enslaved.

Free the Slaves
https://www.freetheslaves.net

Ted Talk with Kevin Bales
http://www.ted.com/speakers/kevin_bales.html

Free the Captives (Houston)
http://www.freethecaptiveshouston.com/

Search for an article about slavery that is happening today.

בְּשַׁלַּח BE·SHALLAH

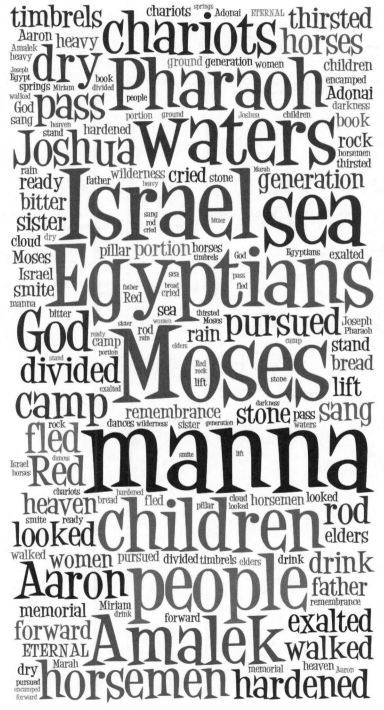

timbrels chariots springs Adonai ETERNAL thirsted horses
Aaron heavy chariots horses children
Amalek heavy ground generation women encamped
Joseph dry book Pharaoh Adonai
Egypt springs Miriam divided people darkness
walked portion ground Joshua children book
God pass heaven stand waters rock
sang hardened horsemen thirsted
Joshua Israel sea
rain father wilderness cried stone Marah generation
ready Israel heavy sea
bitter sang rod bitter
sister pillar portion horses God Egyptians exalted
cloud dry Egyptians exalted
Moses Red sea bread pass fled
Israel sea thirsted Moses
smite father Moses Joseph
manna bitter sister women rain pursued Pharaoh
God ready rod camp stand
camp portion elders bread
divided stand Red rock lift stone lift
exalted Moses
camp remembrance stone pass sang
rock dances wilderness sister generation waters
fled manna smite lift
Israel dances darkness
horses Red heaven bread fled pillar cloud horsemen looked
smite ready children rod
looked chariots hardened looked elders
walked women pursued divided timbrels elders drink drink
Aaron people father
memorial Miriam forward remembrance
forward drink exalted
ETERNAL Amalek walked
dry Marah memorial heaven Aaron
pursued horsemen hardened
encamped forward

Overview: Exodus 13:17—17:16

After the tenth plague Pharaoh finally lets the people of Israel go. As they flee Pharaoh has a change of heart and chases after them. God and Moses split the Reed Sea so the Families-of-Israel can cross on dry land. As the Egyptian army approaches, the sea settles and the Egyptians drown. On the other side of the sea the people of Israel sing the Song of the Sea in celebration. Traveling through the desert is hard for the Families-of-Israel, and they complain bitterly. In order to bring water to the people, Moses hits a rock, and water flows. God provides manna so the people won't be hungry. The people of Israel fight Amalek, who becomes a sworn enemy of our nation.

OUR TORAH TEXT: EXODUS 16:29

In this *sidrah* we meet manna, the miracle food that falls like dew every night to feed the Families-of-Israel in the wilderness. The daily manna collection conflicts with the rules of Shabbat and causes some disagreement. Our verse comes from the middle of this situation, but you'll understand it better if you open a *Tanakh* and read all of Exodus 16 first.

רְאוּ כִּי־יי נָתַן לָכֶם הַשַּׁבָּת עַל־כֵּן הוּא נֹתֵן לָכֶם
בַּיּוֹם הַשִּׁשִּׁי לֶחֶם יוֹמָיִם שְׁבוּ אִישׁ תַּחְתָּיו
אַל־יֵצֵא אִישׁ מִמְּקֹמוֹ בַּיּוֹם הַשְּׁבִיעִי.

ראו כי יי נתן השבת על כן הוא נתן
לכם ביום הששי לחם יומים שבו
איש תחתיו אל יצא איש ממקמו
ביום השביעי

They saw that the Eternal gave them Shabbat for which the Eternal gave to them on the sixth day bread for two days, a person could sit and not go out from his or her place on the seventh day.

Exploring Our Text: The Meaning Of Shabbat

MORDECHAI M. KAPLAN

An artist cannot be continually wielding his brush. He must stop at times in his painting to freshen his vision of the object, the meaning of which he wishes to express on his canvas. Living is also art. We dare not become absorbed in its technical processes and lose our consciousness of its general plan...

The Shabbat represents those moments when we pause in our brushwork to renew our vision of this object. Having done so, we take ourselves to our painting with clarified vision and renewed energy. This applies to the individual and to the community alike.

ABRAHAM JOSHUA HESCHEL

Judaism is a religion of time, aiming at the sanctification of time. Unlike the space-minded man to whom time is unvaried, iterative, homogeneous, to whom all hours are alike, qualitiless, empty shells, the Bible senses the diversified character of time. There are no two hours alike. Every hour is unique and the only one given at the moment, exclusive and endlessly precious.

Judaism teaches us to be attached to holiness in time, to be attached to sacred events, to learn how to consecrate sanctuaries that emerge from the magnificent stream of a year. The Sabbaths are our great cathedrals; and our Holy of Holies is a shrine that neither the Romans nor the Greeks were able to burn....

The meaning of the Sabbath is to celebrate time rather than space. Six days a week we live under the tyranny of things of space; on the Sabbath we try to become attuned to the holiness of time. It is a day on which we are called to share in that which is eternal in time, to turn from the world of creation to the creation of the world (excerpted from *The Sabbath*).

ERIC FROMM

The Sabbath seems to have been an old Babylonian holy day, celebrated every seventh day (*Shapatu*). But its meaning was quite different from that of the biblical Sabbath. The *Babylonian Shapatu* was a day of mourning and self-castigation. It was a somber day, dedicated to the planet Saturn (our "Saturday" is still, in its name, devoted to Saturn—Saturn's Day), whose wrath one wanted to placate by self-castigation and self-punishment.

Saturn (in the old astrological and metaphysical tradition) symbolizes time. He is the god of time and hence the god of death. Inasmuch as man is like God, gifted with a soul, with reason, love and freedom, he is not subject to time or death. But inasmuch as man is an animal, with a body subject to the laws of nature, he is a slave to time and death. The Babylonians sought to appease the lord of time by self-castigation.

The Bible in its Sabbath concept makes an entirely new attempt to solve the problem: by stopping interference with nature for one day you eliminate time; where there is no change, no work, no human interference, there is no time. Instead of a Sabbath on which man bows down to the lord of time, the biblical Sabbath symbolizes man's victory over time; time is suspended, Saturn is dethroned on his very day, Saturn's Day (*The Forgotten Language*, pp. 242 ff.).

Why is Shabbat such an important mitzvah?

torah experience
shabbat dinner table

Create a Shabbat dinner table with the class (make *hallah*, review blessings for candles, wine, *hallah*), and invite Kaplan, Heschel and Fromm to dinner. Each should come dressed in character. They will lead a discussion about the meaning of Shabbat and encourage the students to create statements of personal meaning. Students can play Kaplan, Heschel and Fromm, or you can invite guests to play these roles.

Reflection Question: How do you renew yourself?

MITZVAH OF THE WEEK: שְׁמִירַת שַׁבָּת OBSERVING SABBATH

(1) Sowing (literally "he who sows," and similarly with others); (2) plowing; (3) reaping; (4) binding sheaves; (5) threshing; (6) winnowing; (7) sorting; (8) grinding; (9) sifting; (10) kneading; (11) baking; (12) shearing wool; (13) bleaching it; (14) beating it; (15) dyeing it; (16) spinning; (17) stretching the warp on the loom; (18) making two loops; (19) weaving two threads; (20) separating two threads; (21) tying a knot; (22) untying a knot; (23) sewing two stitches; (24) tearing in order to se two stitches; (25) trapping a deer; (26) slaughtering it; (27) flaying it; (28) salting it; (29) curing its hide; (30) scraping it; (31) cutting it up; (32) writing two letters; (33) erasing in order to write two letters; (34) building; (35) pulling down; (36) putting out a fire; (37) lighting a fire; (38) striking with a hammer (giving the finishing blow with a hammer); and (39) carrying from one place to another.

NOTE: These thirty-nine main classes of work are those that were actually involved with the construction of the Mishkan, and can be divided into the following seven categories: (1) the first eleven deal with the preparation of bread, beginning with plowing and concluding with baking. (2) The next thirteen deal with the manufacture of a garment, from shearing the wool until the final sewing of the stitches. (3) The following nine are connected with writing, from the hunting of a gazelle for procuring the parchment until the actual inscription of the letters. (4) The construction of a building including pulling it down. (5) Lighting a fire and extinguishing it. (6) Completion of a labor, classified as striking with a hammer, and (7) Carrying from one domain to another.

The basic idea, however, is simple. God created and made things for six days and then rested on the seventh day. Shabbat is when we are like God. Six days we are like God. Six day we make things, manipulate and try to change the world. We use nature for our own purposes. On Shabbat we leave the world alone and change nothing—rather we let creation change us. Simply put, these thirty-nine kinds of work are all involved in using and changing nature; resting is leaving creation alone and just experiencing it.

Shabbat Experience

Discuss in a small group.

What set of Shabbat rules does your synagogue/Jewish school teach?

If your family were to adopt a set of Shabbat rules in order to create a time that is different from the rest of the week, what would they be? How do you interpret "Don't work on Shabbat"?

Shabbat Resources

Jews usually name Shabbatot by their Torah portions. There are a couple of special Shabbatot that come from the calendar. In the modern world, organizations create special Shabbatot based on themes. Here are two.

Human Rights Shabbat

http://www.truah.org/resources/human-rights-shabbat.html

Shabbat Across America and Canada

http://njop.org/partners/programs/shabbat-across-america-and-canada/

Find a blog entry that talks about a Shabbat experience.

יִתְרוֹ YITRO

Overview: Exodus 18:1—20:26

Jethro (in Hebrew, *Yitro*), Moses' father-in-law, hears about Moses and all that God has done for the people of Israel and takes Tzipporah, Moses' wife, as well as Gershon and Eliezer, his sons, to see Moses in the desert. Jethro immediately sees how stressed Moses is, since he is leading the people physically and spiritually and acting as the sole judge for the community. Jethro suggests he appoint judges and organize a judicial system. Moses takes his father-in-law's advice and allows Jethro to set up the courts and judiciary system before he leaves. The people of Israel are charged to become "a kingdom of priests and holy people," and Moses tells them to prepare to see God. Moses goes up Mt. Sinai and receives the Ten Commandments.

rejoiced hundreds Moses words hear encamped Remember wilderness ETERNAL horn teach God guiltless Israel encamped ETERNAL mother sake wilderness murder words Yitro encamped delivered mount Israel seventh Zipporah witness jealous people fourth father Midian horn people kissed exceeding sake stand priests mercy father help teach stand God delivered guiltless holy Moses hear steal sake hate gates covet welfare Sabbath adultery thunders rested heard delivered heard help labor daughter make gates heaven generation covenant help priests God make visiting image blessed counsel ass spoken travail heard voice children hallowed welfare people holy ox fourth vain voice tens ass covet loud false holy kissed generation priests love ox covet love cloud father small vain labor loud blessed bowed rejoiced daughter Yitro steal travail stranger Israel wilderness commandments cloud Yitro Sabbath bowed jealous kissed inquire false Midian heaven fifties mercy hallowed stranger judge goodness seasons commit statutes nation cloud Zipporah rested image witness mount Midian mother bondage seventh stand travail generation goodness judge statutes mount commit commandments Sabbath stranger

OUR TORAH TEXT: EXODUS 20:12

In the middle of the Ten Commandments we find:

כַּבֵּד אֶת־אָבִיךָ וְאֶת־אִמֶּךָ לְמַעַן יַאֲרִכוּן יָמֶיךָ
עַל הָאֲדָמָה אֲשֶׁר־יי אֱלֹהֶיךָ נֹתֵן לָךְ.

כבד את אביך ואת אמך למען יראכון
ימיך על אדמה אשר יי אלהיך נתן
לך

Honor your father and your mother that your days may be long on the land that the Eternal your God gives you.

Exploring Our Torah Text

Here is a list of ways of *honoring* and *acting with awe* that later Rabbis added to the literature. Read each one and see if you can add your own suggestions for ways to act.

[1] Children should not raise their voices or speak angrily or sarcastically to their parents (*Pele Yoez*, section *Dibur*).

[2] Children should consider their parents to be distinguished, even if they are not considered distinguished by others (*Sefer Hayyai Adam* 67:3).

[3] Children must not contradict their parent (*Yoreh De'ah* 240:1). If your parent tells you to do something foolish, you must do it (unless it is contrary to Torah) even if your parent will not actually derive pleasure from it. Failure to do as requested is considered contradicting your parent (*Sefer Ha-Makneh* to *Kidushin* 31b; see *Biur ha-Gra* 240:36 and *Tshuvot Rav Akiva Eiger* 68).

[4] Children must not call parents by name (*Yoreh De'ah* 240:1).

[5] Children should serve parents with a pleasant facial expression; for if they serve them with a dismal face, it is wrong.…A person's attitude and manner of speaking to his parents are what counts *(Yoreh De'ah 240:4)*.

[6] When children study Torah and are well behaved, it is an honor for their parents *(Yoma 86a; Zevah Mishpachah, p. 26)*.

[7] Children have no right to humiliate or embarrass parents, regardless of what they do. If a parent takes a wallet full of money and throws it into the sea, the child must not humiliate or grow angry at the parent. Rather, the child must accept the Torah's decree and remain silent. There is a halakhic opinion that if a parent wants to throw away a child's money, the child has a right to prevent this. But after the parent has thrown the money away the child has no right to insult his parent but does have the right to make a claim against the parent in court *(Yoreh De'ah 240:8)*.

[8] Parents must not act cruelly toward their children nor needlessly cause them anguish *(Sefer ha-Brit, part 2, no. 13)*. Parents are forbidden to burden children excessively or to be overly concerned about their respect for them, for this would constitute a stumbling block. Rather, parents should forgive children and overlook things, for a parent has a right to forgo honor *(Yoreh De'ah 240:19)*.

[9] If a mother tells her child to do a specific act and afterward the father angrily asks him, "Why did you do this?" the child should not reveal that this was the mother's wish *(Sefer Hasidim 336)*.

[10] You fulfill the commandment of honoring your parents whenever you fulfill any of their wishes *(Sefer Hasidim 152)*. Honoring your parents' relatives is considered as honoring your parents *(Sheurim Ha-Metzuyanim B'Halakhah, vol. 4, p. 31)*. A person is obligated to honor his or her parents even after they die, and for this reason children say *Kaddish* for a deceased parent *(Hayyai Adam 67)*.

This list was drawn from *Love Your Neighbor*, Zelig Pliskin, Aish HaTorah Press.

What other guidelines for how to act would you add to this list?

torah experience

Look at these three sTalmudic examples of how we can honor our parents.

[1] Blessing one's father and mother is the same as blessing God…This comparison makes sense because fathers, mothers and God are partners in the creation of every child. The Holy One says, "When people honor their fathers and mothers, I consider it as if I had lived among them and they had honored Me."

[2] Rabbi Ulla taught, "When the Holy One taught the first two of the Ten Commandments—'I am The Eternal your God' and 'You shall not have other gods before Me'—the nations of the world reacted poorly. They said, 'Your God is being selfish. Your God is only saying this out of arrogance.' But when God then commanded, 'Honor your father and your mother,' they changed their minds and acknowledged the wisdom of the Ten Commandments."

[3] Rabbi Tarfon had an elderly mother whom he treated with respect. Whenever she wanted to climb into bed, he would bend down and she would climb onto him and into the bed; and whenever she descended from the bed, she would descend onto him to reach the floor.

Work in a group. Act out a good example of a real time when someone honored his or her parent.

Reflection Question: When is it harder to honor your parents?

MITZVAH OF THE WEEK: כַּבֵּד אֶת־אָבִיךָ וְאֶת־אִמֶּךָ HONORING PARENTS

The Torah tells us on multiple occasions that we are to honor our parents.

Honor your father and your mother (Exodus 20:12).

Each person should be in awe of his or her mother and father (Leviticus 19:3).

In the Talmud the rabbis explore the difference between these two mitzvot.

What is **awe** and what is **honor**?

Awe means that a son must neither stand nor sit in his father's place, nor contradict his words, nor side with his opponent in an argument.

Honor means that a son must give his father food and drink, and clothe and cover him. (*Kiddushin* 32a)

In your own words, what is the difference between awe and honor?

Kabed Et Avikha V'et Imekha Experience

Hold a debate.

Resolved: The child of an abusive parent should not be obligated to honor that parent.

Reflection Question: When is it hardest to honor one or both of your parents?

Kabed et Avikha v'et Imekha Resources

Here are a number of responsa that answer our case.

The Institue for Dayyanim (Orthodox)
http://www.dinonline.org/2011/01/28/honoring-abusive-parents/

Rabbinical Assembly (Conservative)
https://www.rabbinicalassembly.org/sites/default/files/public/
halakhah/teshuvot/19912000/dorff_violence.pdf

CCAR (Reform)
http://ccarnet.org/responsa/arr-139-141/

Jewish Values Online
http://www.jewishvaluesonline.org/question.
php?id=132&cprg=%2Fsearch.php%3Fsubcatid%3D23%20
http://www.jewishvaluesonline.org/question.
php?id=132&cprg=%2Fsearch.php%3Fsubcatid%3D23

No Reconstructionist responsa could be found.

Find three URLs that show you how to respect parents.

שפטים MISHPATIM

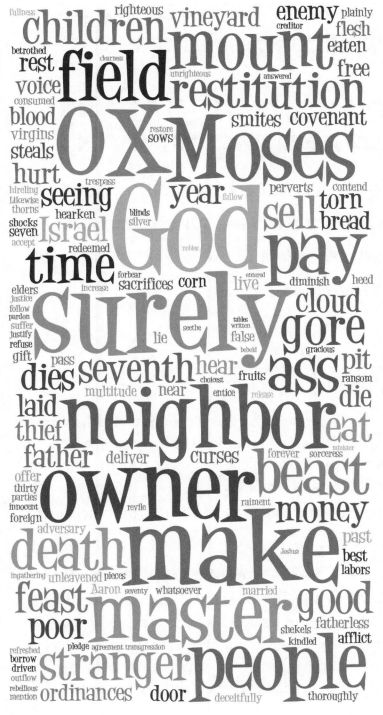

children righteous vineyard enemy plainly
fullness creditor flesh
betrothed mount eaten
rest field clearness free
voice unrightness answered
consumed restitution
blood ox smites covenant
virgins restore sows
steals Moses
hurt seeing year fallow torn
hireling blinds sell bread
Likewise hearken silver
thorns Israel God pay
shocks redeemed nobles
seven accept
time sacrifices corn live diminish heed
elders entered cloud
justice surely tables gore
follow lie seethe written
pardon false beheld gracious
suffer
justify pass pit
refuse dies seventh hear ass ransom
gift multitude near choicest fruits release die
laid entice
thief neighbor eat
father deliver curses forever sorceress minister
offer revile beast
thirty raiment money
parties owner past
innocent Joshua best
foreign adversary labors
death make
ingathering unleavened pieces
feast Aaron seventy whatsoever married good
poor master fatherless
shekels kindled afflict
refreshed pledge agreement transgression
borrow stranger people
driven
outflow ordinances door deceitfully thoroughly
rebellious
mention

**Overview:
Exodus
21:1—24:18**

After announcing the core Ten Commandments, God has Moses teach the Jewish people a basic law code that elaborates on what they've already heard. It includes criminal law, civil law (rules for owning slaves, personal injury, property damage, etc.), ethical commands (laws forbidding the oppression of the powerless, mitzvah of lending to the poor and other social codes), and ritual law (laws of the sabbatical year, Shabbat and festivals). The Families-of-Israel accept the law, and Moses goes up Mt. Sinai alone to receive the stone tablets, remaining there for forty days and nights.

OUR TORAH TEXT: EXODUS 22:24

Parashat Mishpatim is a law code. According to *Sefer ha-Hinukh* it contains fifty-three mitzvot. We've chosen a verse that generates three of these mitzvot, all of which have to do with lending money and interest.

אִם־כֶּסֶף תַּלְוֶה אֶת־עַמִּי אֶת־הֶעָנִי עִמָּךְ
לֹא־תִהְיֶה לוֹ כְּנֹשֶׁה לֹא־תְשִׂמוּן עָלָיו נֶשֶׁךְ.

אִם לסף תלוה את עמי את העני עמך
לא תהיה לו כנשה לא תשמון עליו נשך

If you lend money to any of My people, even the poor that are with you, you should not act toward him/her as a creditor, nor shall you charge him/her interest.

Exploring Our Torah Text

Use the text that is already there as a resource to debate the value in the Jewish loan system. Bring information about interest in American loans to class so students can compare/contrast the different systems.

Here are four excerpts from *Sefer ha-Hinukh* that teach laws regarding loans.

Exodus 22:24: If you lend money to my people, even the poor that are with you... It is a mitzvah to lend money to a poor man in order to lighten his burden and relieve his anguish. This mitzvah is even greater than the mitzvah of giving charity. For by accepting a loan, the unfortunate person can be helped in a dignified manner, whereas those who receive charity experience some degree of shame.

Exodus 22:24: You shall not act toward him/her as a creditor... We are forbidden to demand payment of a loan from a borrower at a time when we know that she lacks the means with which to pay her debt. The purpose of this mitzvah is that we firmly implant in our hearts the qualities of kindness and compassion for another person.

Exodus 22:24: You shall not charge him/her interest... We are forbidden to assist or support in any way a borrower or a lender in transacting a loan with interest. Besides the lender and borrower, the scribe, guarantor and witnesses are also forbidden to take part in a transaction involving a loan with interest.

Deuteronomy 23:20: You shall not pay your brother interest. It is forbidden to borrow money at interest from a Jew. This mitzvah prohibits the borrower from paying interest, while other mitzvot prohibit the lender from accepting interest.

Based on these four laws, what should a Jew do when he or she is asked to lend money to another Jew?

Why is this law important enough to repeat?

torah experience

Break into groups of three. Have each member of each group create a loan application for $5,000 from a free loan society. Have each group of three pair with another group of three. One group presents their loan stories. The other group sits as the officials of the free loan society. While the group has $15,000 in requests, they have only $8,000 to loan. Work through the process, then switch.

Reflection Question: What does one do when the need is greater than the funds available?

MITZVAH OF THE WEEK: לֹא־תְשִׂמוּן עָלָיו נֶשֶׁךְ LENDING BUT NOT CHARGING INTEREST

Our Torah verse has caused Jews to create a series of free loan societies that help the poor. This is an idea that the world has adopted. The Grameen Bank, considered the first modern microcredit institution, was founded in 1976 by Muhammad Yunus. He was awarded the Nobel Peace Prize in 2006 for his work providing microcredit services to the poor.

Why is it important for Jews to make loans but not charge interest? What does this say about the way we handle money? Value the lender? Value the borrower?

Lo T'simun Neshekh Experience

Research free loan societies and create a P.S.A. (public service announcement) for them.

Reflection Question: What system makes more sense to you, the one set up by the rabbis or the American system? Why?

Lo T'simun Neshekh Resources

Here are websites for both free loan and microlending institutions.

Hebrew Free Loan Society
http://www.hfls.org/

Finca
http://www.finca.org

Kiva Loans
http://www.kiva.org/

Jewish Free Loan Association
http://www.jfla.org/

Compare and contrast them.

Find three other websites that work on preserving the dignity of the poor while helping them.

תְּרוּמָה TERUMAH

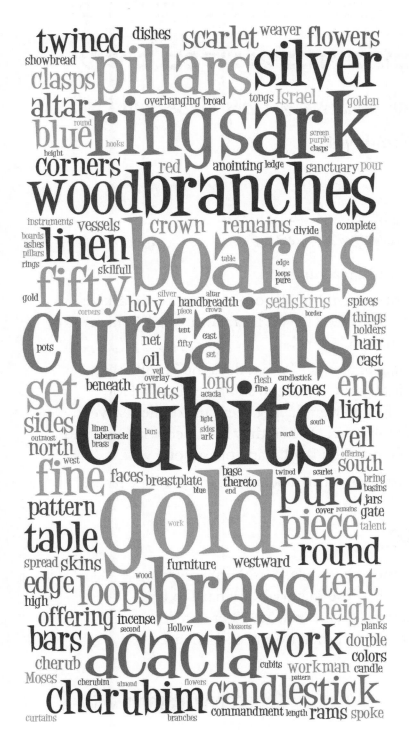

twined dishes scarlet weaver flowers
showbread pillars silver
clasps overhanging broad tongs Israel golden
altar rings ark
blue round hooks screen purple clasps
corners red anointing ledge sanctuary pour
wood branches
instruments vessels crown remains divide complete
boards
linen boards
ashes pillars table edge loops pure
rings
gold fifty skilfull silver altar sealskins spices
holy handbreadth piece crown border things
pots curtains holders
net tent hair
oil fifty set cast
candlestick
long flesh stones end
set beneath fillets acacia fine light
sides light sides ark veil
outmost linen bars south north
north tabernacle brass offering
west cubits south
fine faces breastplate base twined scarlet bring
pattern blue thereto end pure basins
table work cover remains jars
gold piece gate talent
spread skins round
edge loops furniture westward brass tent
high wood height
offering incense blossoms planks
bars acacia work double
cherub second Hollow cubits workman candle
Moses almond flowers pattern colors
cherubim candlestick
curtains branches commandment length rams spoke

Overview: Exodus 25:1–27:19

God asks Moses to have the Families-of-Israel build a sanctuary so God can dwell in it. Moses calls for volunteers to bring thirteen specific materials they are looking for. Gifts of all sizes are encouraged and welcomed. There are detailed instructions about the ark (*aron*), table (*shulhan*), and lamp (*menorah*).

OUR TORAH TEXT: EXODUS 25:8

In this *sidrah* the Families of Israel begin to build the *Mishkan*, the portable sanctuary used in the wilderness. This verse is the culmination of God's directions.

וְעָשׂוּ לִי מִקְדָּשׁ וְשָׁכַנְתִּי בְּתוֹכָם.

ועשׂו ל מקדשׁ ושׁכנתי בתוכם

And you shall build me a Holy Place and I will hang out among you.

Exploring Our Torah Text

This is a Hasidic teaching.

> Rabbi Menahem Mendle of Kotzk was once asked: "Where does God live?' His answer was, "Wherever a person lets God in."

> The *Nahalat Shiv'ah*: "What does the Torah mean when it teaches, "And you shall build me a Holy Place"? He answered, "Let them make themselves into a Holy Place. When they are filled with awe and love of God, then I will hang out among you."

Work with a partner and discuss: "How can a person become a holy place?"

tORAH eXPerIeNCe

Research and build a model of the Tabernacle (Mishkan) according to the instructions in the *parashah*. If the materials are hard to find, have the students draw architectural plans instead. There are lots of plans and reconstructions on the internet. (Many of them are Christian.)

Reflection Question: When are you a holy place?

MITZVAH OF THE WEEK: עֲשׂוּ לִי מִקְדָּשׁ MAKING A SANCTUARY

It is a mitzvah to build a house for God's sake. This house (*Beit ha-Mikdash*) is where we offer our sacrifices to God, and it is to this holy site that we are commanded to ascend for the pilgrimage festivals every year.

In this day and age, when there is no longer a single Temple in Jerusalem, this sense of holiness is transferred to the synagogue sanctuary. In the Mishnah (*Megillah* chapter 3) we find the rules for keeping holy the space where Jews study and worship.

1. If the people of a town have sold an open space, they may purchase a synagogue with its proceeds. If they have sold a synagogue, they may purchase an ark. If they have sold an ark, they may buy Torah mantles. If they have sold Torah mantles, they may buy books. If they have sold books, they may purchase a scroll of the Law. But if they sold a scroll of the Law, they may not buy books. If they have sold books, they must not buy mantles. If they have sold mantles, they may not purchase an ark. If they have sold an ark, they may not buy a synagogue. If they have sold a synagogue, they may not purchase an open space.

2. They may sell a synagogue except for four purposes: for a bathhouse, for a tannery, for a ritual bath, or for a urinal.

3. R. Judah said, "If a synagogue be derelict, they may not deliver a funeral oration therein, nor may they twist ropes therein, nor may they spread nets therein, nor spread out produce upon its roof, nor make of it a short-cut."

What are the rules for a holy space?

According to this Mishnah, what makes a space holy?

What do you think makes a space holy?

How is your sanctuary holy?

How do you act differently in a holy space? Why or why not?

V'Asu Li Mikdash Experience

my body...
is my temple...

walk the halls of me...
leave Your footprints
across my floor plan and

take Your seat upon the throne...
calling my temple Your palace...
make it Your home... (anonymous)

Trace your body on a sheet of butcher paper (you will need help). Yes, this is like what you did in kindergarten or first grade. This time draw the floor plan of your body as a temple. Share it first with a friend, then with the whole class.

V'Asu Li Mikdash Resources

All of these organizations help people with medical problems. **Hadassah** runs some of the best hospitals in Israel—some of the best hospitals in the world. **Magen David Adom** is the Jewish equivalent of the Red Cross. **Yad Sarah** is an non-profit organization in Israel that provides medical equipment for people in need of help. They have helped half the families in Israel.

Hadassah Medical Center
http://www.hadassah-med.com/about.aspx

Magen David Adom
http://www.mdais.com/

Yad Sarah
http://www.yadsarah.org

Find another site that helps to treat people as if they are created in God's image.

מצוה TETZAVEH

gold holy statute pomegranate
commanded remain covers woven
crown dash blood
consecration Aaron wheaten linen
sons ram
head breastplate
Aaron
offering fine
anoint mitre gird office
children
priest tunic ends
stones altar rings
atonement
tent garments robe
purple ephod work bullock
blue Israel engravings

Overview:
Exodus
27:20—30:10

The construction of the Tabernacle is described in more detail, this time for the eternal flame (*ner tamid*), the oil (*shemen*) and the priestly garments, including the tunic, pants, belt, hat, apron, breastplate and headplate. We read about the special ceremony for the priests, which lasts seven days and includes sacrifices, ritual washing and more. Aaron and his sons (Nadav, Avihu, Eleazar and Itamar) are chosen to be priests.

OUR TORAH TEXT: EXODUS 27:20

In this *parashah* we continue with the description of the holy items that will be needed to worship in the *Mishkan*. Our verse focuses on a small detail: the olive oil burned in the menorah.

וְאַתָּה תְּצַוֶּה אֶת-בְּנֵי יִשְׂרָאֵל וְיִקְחוּ אֵלֶיךָ
שֶׁמֶן זַיִת זָךְ כָּתִית לַמָּאוֹר לְהַעֲלֹת נֵר תָּמִיד.

ואתה תצוה את בני ישראל ויקזזו
אליך שמן זית זך כתית למאור
להעלת נר תמיד

And you shall command the Families-of-Israel that they should take beaten olive oil to light up the ner tamid.

Exploring our Torah Text

In the midrash on this passage they quote another verse from Proverbs:

> The commandment is a lamp, and the teaching is light (Prov. 6:23).

In the midrash the rabbis use this verse to give a symbolic meaning to the mitzvah of the *ner tamid*, a parable of one who stands in a dark place. No sooner does he or she start walking than he or she stumbles over a stone or comes to a gutter and falls into it, striking the ground with her/his face. Why does this happen? Because the person has no light in his or her hand. So it is with the unlearned person who possesses no Torah. When he or she comes upon a transgression, he or she stumbles and dies. But they who study Torah give light wherever they are. A parable: One stands in the dark with a lamp in his hand. When he or she comes upon a stone, he or she does not stumble over it; when he or she comes upon a gutter, he or she does not fall into it. Why not? Because he or she has a lamp in his or her hand, as Torah says, "Your word (Torah) is a lamp to my feet, and a light to my path." *(Exodus Rabbah 36.3)*

What is the symbolic meaning the rabbis give to the *ner tamid*?

TORAH EXPERIENCE

Listen to "Light One Candle" by Peter Yarrow. Here is a video of him singing it with Paul and Mary.

http://www.youtube.com/watch?v=3yZ1zxtbOJE

What symbolic meaning for the *Ner Tamid* can you draw from this song?

Reflection Question: What is your *Ner Tamid*?

MITZVAH OF THE WEEK: נֵר תָּמִיד AN EVERLASTING FLAME

It is a mitzvah for the *Kohanim* to kindle the menorah in the *Beit ha-Mikdash* every evening. This mitzvah also includes discarding old wicks, removing the ashes, cleaning the oil cups and refilling them with sufficient oil to burn through the night.

This mitzvah can't be done today because there is no longer a Temple in Jerusalem. In its place is a *zekher mitzvah,* a practice we do to remember the original mitzvah. Describe what we do to remember this mitzvah.

This is a mitzvah we can also do symbolically. List seven things we can do to keep the *ner tamid* burning.

Ner Tamid Experience

Darken your room. Sit in a circle. Place a candle in the middle. As a class, make a list of things that should be eternal like the *ner tamid*.

Reflection Question: What do you believe is the number one thing that should be eternal?

Ner Tamid Resources

National Conference of Shomrim Societies started as *Ner Tamid*. It is an organization for Jewish policemen and firemen.

Shomrim
http://www.nationalshomrim.org

Find another kind of organization that uses the title "Shomrim".

כי תשא KiTiSSA

Overview: Exodus 30:11–34:35

God instructs Moses how to take (the first-ever) census. Through this census all men (twenty and over) are required to pay a tax of one half shekel to support the Tabernacle. Betzalel is appointed the master craftsman of the entire Tabernacle. God restates the rules of Shabbat. We then return to Moses on top of Mt. Sinai receiving the Ten Commandments from God. Down below the people are uneasy and worried about where Moses has gone. To calm them, Aaron asks for people to bring gold, and they create a golden calf for the people to worship. When Moses returns from the top of the mountain he is so angered by the idol that he smashes the tablets. Moses goes up to get a second set of tablets after punishing the Families-of-Israel.

103

OUR TORAH TEXT: EXODUS 34:26

In the middle of the Tabernacle rules the Torah does a flashback to Moses getting laws and bringing down the two tablets of the Law. In the middle of a short law code we find this rule:

לֹא־תְבַשֵּׁל גְּדִי בַּחֲלֵב אִמּוֹ.

לא תבשל גדי בחלב אמו

You shall not boil a baby goat in its mother's milk.

Exploring Our Torah Text

Neither the Bible nor the Talmud explains why milk and meat cannot be mixed. Maimonides explains the origin as a Jewish disgust at the fertility rites practiced by the pagan cults of Canaan *(Guide to the Perplexed 3:48)*. One of these rites was the cooking of a kid in its mother's milk. Dr. Nelson Glueck reports that this practice is still found among the Bedouin of today, not as a pagan rite but as an act of hospitality to a distinguished guest.

To us this regulation reflects reverence for life and the teaching of compassion. To boil a kid in its mother's milk is callous. Professor Abraham Joshua Heschel expresses it thus: "The goat—in our case, more commonly the cow—generously and steadfastly provides man with the single most perfect food that she possesses, milk. It is the only food which, by reason of its proper composition of fat, carbohydrates, and protein, can by itself sustain the human body. How ungrateful and callous we would be to take the child of an animal to whom we are thus indebted and cook it in the very milk which nourishes us and is given us so freely by its mother" (Dresner and Siegel, *Jewish Dietary Laws*, p. 70).

Klein, *Jewish Religious Practice*

What sense can you make of this commandment?

torah experience

Debate *kashrut* in class (various religious perspectives: Reform, Conservative, Orthodox, ethical vegetarians).

Resolved: "Jews no longer need to keep kosher."

Or have a presentation from local rabbis or *mashgihim*, if possible a *shohet*.

Reflection Question: Does anything about eating connect you to God?

MITZVAH OF THE WEEK: לֹא־תְבַשֵּׁל גְּדִי בַּחֲלֵב אִמּוֹ
YOU SHALL NOT COOK A KID IN ITS MOTHER'S MILK

You shall not cook a kid in its mother's milk. It is forbidden to eat meat and milk that were cooked together. This prohibition is different from other forbidden foods, for even if one does not benefit from it while eating it, he is liable.

It is customary to place special marks on dairy and meat utensils and flatware, to differentiate between them and make them easily recognizable. A pot in which meat and milk were cooked becomes forbidden until it is purified to make it kosher. Bread that comes in contact with meat may not be eaten with dairy. Similarly, if bread comes in contact with cheese, it may not be eaten with meat.

After eating meat one must wait at least one, three or six hours before eating dairy. However, one may eat meat a short while after eating dairy, provided one thoroughly rinses the mouth and/or brushes his/her teeth, so as not to leave any particles of the dairy food lodged between his/her teeth.

Reflection Question: Do you watch what you eat? What does it do for you?

Kashrut Experience

Write your own responsum for one of two modern *kashrut* dilemmas

1. Several scientific studies say that the way animals are killed to make their meat kosher is not the kindest way. Should Jews give up *kashrut* for a kinder kill?

2. Research shows that a company that produces kosher products treats its employees badly and cheats them. Knowing this, should food from that company still be considered kosher?

Kashrut Resources

There are now a number of organizations that are tying *kashrut* to ethics. "Kosher" really means "fit for Jewish use," and these organizations say that everything about kosher food must be ethical. Temple Grandin is not Jewish, but she is the world's expert on animal feelings, and she teaches about *kashrut*.

Magen Tzedek
http://www.magentzedek.org

Tav ha-Yashar
http://www.utzedek.org/tavhayosher.html

Temple Grandin's Recommended Ritual Slaughter Practices
http://www.grandin.com/ritual/rec.ritual.slaughter.html

Find out about hoisting and shackling (this is a big issue in kashrut *kindness).*

ויקהל VA-YAK'HEL

Overview:
Exodus
35:1–38:20

Moses continues teaching about the rules of Shabbat and the building of the *Mishkan*. The actual work of building the *Mishkan* is described—the ark, the table, the menorah, the altar of incense, the anointing oil, the altar of burnt offering and more. Contributions are needed for the work to begin. The people respond so positively that Moses has to refuse some of the donations. Work begins on the *Mishkan*.

107

OUR TORAH TEXT: EXODUS 35:3

We've already learned the "don't work on Shabbat" rule earlier in the Torah. Now the Torah teaches another Shabbat rule.

לֹא־תְבַעֲרוּ אֵשׁ בְּכֹל מֹשְׁבֹתֵיכֶם בְּיוֹם הַשַּׁבָּת.

לא תבערו אש בכל משבתיכם
ביום השבת

Don't light a fire in any of your households on the Sabbath day.

Exploring Our Torah Text

Traditional Laws of Lighting Shabbat Candles

1. One lights candles before Shabbat begins. The candlelight creates an atmosphere of peace and tranquility in the home.

2. The primary mitzvah is to light candles in the room where the Shabbat meal will be served. There must already be sufficient light in the other rooms of the house that will be used.

3. The mitzvah of lighting the Shabbat candles is principally the woman's. Every member of the household fulfills his mitzvah to light Shabbat candles when the woman lights hers.

4. When there is no woman in the house, the man lights the Shabbat candles.

5. From the moment a woman lights the candles she must observe the rules of Shabbat and stop doing things that are forbidden on Shabbat.

6. After lighting the candles one recites the blessing over the lighting of the Shabbat candle. The woman covers her face with her hands while reciting the blessing.

How do these rules keep us from lighting a fire on Shabbat?

How would you do all the lighting on *Shabbat Hannukah*?

tOrAH exPerience

Make Shabbat bags to deliver (or have congregation mail) to:
- members who cannot attend services
- members in the hospital over Shabbat
- Jews in a hospital or a nursing home
- members in a nursing home

Each bag should include:
- candlesticks and candles (tea lights)
- small bottle of grape juice (a juice box can suffice)
- mini-hallah
- Shabbat blessings card
- note from the student arranging the bag

Reflection Question: Name some birthday party rules. Why are these rules important to having a good birthday party? Why are rules important to Shabbat?

MITZVAH OF THE WEEK: לֹא־תְבַעֲרוּ אֵשׁ NOT LIGHTING A FIRE ON SHABBAT

Our Torah text forbids lighting fires on Shabbat. In contemporary Jewish law the firing of a spark plug in a car and the use of electricity are considered to be violations of Jewish law.

Lo Tivaru Aish Experience

Here are some test cases for this law. Put a T next to those items that are permitted under traditional Jewish law. Put an ✗ next to those activities that Conservative Judaism allows. Because Reform Judaism believes that individuals should make their own decisions about Shabbat observance, put an ✓ next to any of these activities that you would allow.

- ☐ Driving to synagogue for services.
- ☐ Driving to the woods to enjoy nature.
- ☐ Driving a friend to the emergency room.
- ☐ Leaving the kitchen light on all Shabbat.
- ☐ Turning the light bulb in the refrigerator on and off each time the door is opened.
- ☐ Turning the lights on and off with a Shabbat clock.
- ☐ Turning the television on and off with a Shabbat clock.
- ☐ Turning on the television to watch a cultural program.

Here are a few legal texts to help you work out the official positions on these cases.

> Most modern travel is by car. It is often claimed that driving requires less effort than walking, but in fact, it is easy to find halakhic reasons to avoid driving on Shabbat. First there is the prohibition against creating fire. Even according to the opinion that electricity is not fire, actual fire is created in the engine of the car (Klein, *A Guide to Jewish Ritual Practice*).

> If someone is trapped in a building that has collapsed, you are allowed to violate the Sabbath to dig for him. If at first you find only dead bodies, you must continue digging for as long as there is a little bit of hope that one person is alive (*Yoma* 8:5).

> Under the conditions of our day, many congregants live far from the synagogue and cannot attend services unless they ride. For many of these people, attendance at services is their only contact

with religious life…therefore it is our considered opinion that the positive value involved in the participation in public worship on the Sabbath outweighs the negative value of refraining from riding in an automobile….every other alternative must be exhausted first (The Law Committee of the Rabbinical Assembly).

Be like the rabbis. Think of five other things we might learn from the "no fire on Shabbat" rule:

1. _____
2. _____
3. _____
4. _____
5. _____

Reflection Question: What are your family's Shabbat rules? What would you add to them?

Lo Tivaru Aish Resources

Here are some Shabbat–based organizations. Some hook Jews up with other Jews to celebrate Shabbat. Others sponsor special Shabbatot.

Shabbat.com
http://www.shabbat.com

Oneg Shabbat.org
http://www.oneg-shabbat.org/

Global Hunger Shabbat
http://ajws.org/reversehunger/ghs.html

Freedom Shabbat
http://www.freedomshabbat.org/

Find a website that gives Shabbat recipes.

פְקוּדֵי PEKUDEI

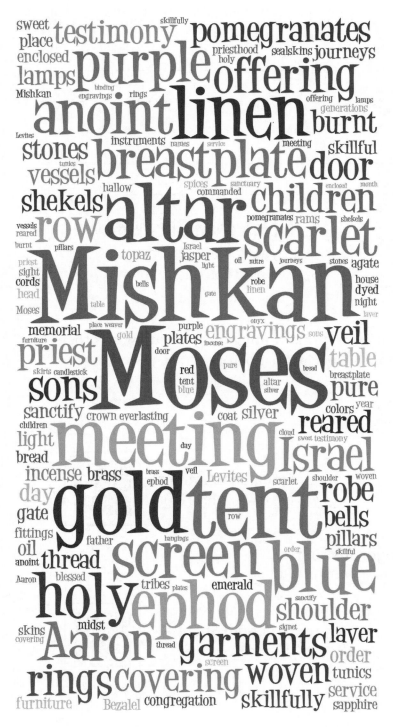

Moses reports how the donations were given for the *Mishkan* and how they were used. He sets up the *Mishkan* and establishes the priests in it. The book of Exodus ends with the description of the cloud that covers the *Mishkan* by day and the fire that burns by night, establishing God's presence in the Tabernacle.

OUR TORAH TEXT: EXODUS 40:31

In *Pekudei* the *Mishkan* is finally set up and put into use. As part of that larger event, our verse is one little part!

וְרָחֲצוּ מִמֶּנּוּ מֹשֶׁה וְאַהֲרֹן וּבָנָיו אֶת־יְדֵיהֶם
וְאֶת־רַגְלֵיהֶם.

ורזזצו ממנו משה ואהרן ובניו את
ידיהם ואת רגליהם

And Moses and Aaron and his sons washed their hands and feet from it.

Exploring Our Text

In the *Kitzur Shulhan Arukh* there are pages of rules about how to wash before meals. Read these excerpts.

40.1 Before eating bread over which the brakhah *ha-Motzi* is to be said, one must first wash hands. If the bread is larger than the size of an egg, both the hand-washing and the brakhah are required.

40.2 The water used for ritual hand-washing must be poured out of a vessel that is perfect, one that has neither a crack nor a hole. If it has a spout, we must not pour the water out of the spout.

40.4 There is no precise amount of water that must be poured, but the entire hand up to the wrist must be covered with one outpouring of the water. It is best to pour water twice on each hand to make sure they have been completely covered.

40.5 After the hands have been covered, rub them together and lift them up. Before drying we say the brakhah:

113

Praised are You, Eternal, Our God, Ruler of the Cosmos
Who made us holy with the mitzvot and made it a mitzvah
for us to wash our hands.

41.2 One must be careful not to linger between the washing and the brakhah *ha-Motzi*, but one may say "Amen" to any brakhot that are heard; one doesn't talk or do any other act in between the washing and the saying of *ha-Motzi*.

torah experience

In Judaism, hand-washing has a special significance. In this *parashah* Moses, Aaron and his sons (who are all to become priests) wash their hands and feet. This action makes them ritually pure. Here is the blessing for hand-washing. We say this blessing on *Erev Shabbat* and during the Passover seder.

בָּרוּךְ אַתָּה יי אֱלֹהֵינוּ מֶלֶךְ הָעוֹלָם
אֲשֶׁר קִדְּשָׁנוּ בְּמִצְוֹתָיו וְצִוָּנוּ עַל נְטִילַת יָדַיִם.

Barukh Attah The Eternal, Eloheinu Melekh ha-Olam,
asher kid'shanu b'mitzvotav, v'tzivanu al n'tilat yadayim.

Blessed are You, Eternal, our God, Ruler of the Cosmos, who has sanctified us with mitzvot and made it a mitzvah to wash our hands.

If we are commanded to wash our hands as part of our meal rituals before Shabbat and Passover, and also as part of a ceremony where priests became ritually pure, what kinds of things do you think hand-washing prepares us for?

Regularly cleaning hands is also one of the easiest ways to prevent getting sick. Sometimes we need a reminder! Create signs to hang in the bathrooms around the synagogue for hand-washing. Be sure to include:

- Hebrew blessing with English translation and transliteration
- Reasons for the importance of washing hands, health-wise or Jewish ritual.

Reflection Question: What does clean feel like?

MITZVAH OF THE WEEK: נְטִילַת יָדַיִם RITUAL HAND-WASHING

The official mitzvah here is for the *Kohanim* to wash before performing their rituals. However, there is a direct echo of this mitzvah in daily Jewish practice. The Torah says (Exodus 19:6) that the Jews should be "a nation of *Kohanim* and a holy people." Simultaneously, we know that the table where we dine is like an altar. Therefore, as with priests, it is a Jewish custom to ritually wash before eating.

N'tilat Yadi'im Experience

What is the difference between ritual washing and practical washing? How does ritual washing help you to reach a level of holiness?

Read the rules for hand-washing on pages 113 and 114. Then design a chart on how to wash hands. Clue: It is traditional to use a special cup with two handles.

Reflection Question: What does hand washing mean to you?

N'tilat Yadi'im Resources

Yad in Hebrew means "memorial" and "institution" as well as "hand". Here are some Jewish organizations whose names are based on *yad*.

Yad Vashem
http://www.yadvashem.org/

Yad Eliezer
http://www.yadeliezer.org/

Yad Avraham
http://yadavraham.org/

Yad Hanadiv
http://www.yadhanadiv.org.il/

Use the internet to find the biblical verse that is the origin of Yad VaShem.

וַיִּקְרָא VA-YIKRA

The third book of the Torah, Leviticus, opens with an introduction to the sacrifices. Details are provided for the regular daily offering (the *olah*), the meal offering (the *minhah*) of flour and water, the peace offering (the *shelamim*), the sin offering (*hatat*) and the guilt offering (*asham*).

OUR TORAH TEXT: LEVITICUS 5:1

In the middle of a lot of laws about guilt offerings and other sacrifices comes our verse, which teaches an important lesson about civic responsibility.

נֶפֶשׁ כִּי־תֶחֱטָא וְשָׁמְעָה קוֹל אָלָה וְהוּא עֵד
אוֹ רָאָה אוֹ יָדָע אִם־לוֹא יַגִּיד וְנָשָׂא עֲוֹנוֹ.

נפש כי תחטא ושמעה קול אלה והוא
עד או ראה או ידע אם לוא יגיד
ונשא עונו

If a person sins by hearing a voice, being a witness or being an eavesdropper—if he sees or knows and does not do anything—that is a sin.

Exploring Our Torah Text

The Case of Crebbs vs. Galuf

Note to the teacher: Consider setting up a mock courtroom in the classroom for this activity!

Be Fair! What Is Your Verdict?

In Jewish law we are given these rules for acceptable witness. Read them and see how they would change the case.

A person cannot be found guilty or blamed because of the testimony of just one witness. For every offense, two (or even three) witnesses are needed to establish a verdict (Deuteronomy 19:15).

Ten categories of people are not qualified to serve as witnesses (or judges): women, slaves, minors (under thirteen), the insane, the deaf, the blind, the wicked, the contemptible, relatives and interested (involved) parties *(Yad, Laws of Evidence 9:1)*.

The following are ineligible to be witnesses (or judges): gamblers, loan sharks, grifters *(Sanhedrein 3:3)*.

Also ineligible (to be a witness or a judge) is a friend or an enemy *(Sandhedrien 3:5)*.

> Based on these Jewish rules of evidence, what should be the verdict in the case below?
>
> What important insights into the process of justice are evident by these Jewish rules?
>
> What (if any) value problems do you find with these Jewish rules of evidence?

torah experience

Judge This Case

A man, Robert Galuf, rented a car from Mr. Crebbs' Rent-A-Beaut. He had the car for three days. The day after it was returned Mr. Crebbs' mechanic, Charles X. Kahn, found a large dent in the rear left fender. Mr. Crebbs asked Robert to pay $750 for the damage, but he claims that the dent was there when he picked up the "beaut." The written contract signed by Mr. Galuf showed that he was responsible for any damage to the car, but both he and Mr. Kahn had failed to initial the boxes that showed the car had been inspected prior to leaving the garage. The matter was taken to court. Here is the collected testimony.

Mr. Crebbs: I own a car rental service called Rent-A-Beaut. Our cars are all older used models, but they are all in perfect condition. I personally checked out the 1992 Lincoln that Mr. Galuf rented. It had just been repainted. There wasn't a scratch on it. When it was returned, we found this $750 dent.

Mr. Galuf: When the major rental companies were out of cars, I had to get a car from this Rent-A-Beaut. When I came in to pick up the car I noticed the dent, but the mechanic told me not to worry about it. He said, and I quote, "All our beauts have dents."

Mrs. Galuf: My husband Bob is telling the truth. While I didn't go with him to pick up the car, he complained about the dent and showed it to me as soon as he got back to the hotel.

W. Ino:	1 lost my job about six months ago. I've been living next to a dumpster in an alley across the street from the Rent-A-Beaut lot. On the day that this Mr. Galuf returned the car, I saw a big dent in the left-hand side. I know, 'cause he sped down my alley and almost hit me. I yelled at him, "No wonder your car looks that way!" Then I saw him pull into Rent-A-Beaut.
D. Lemon:	I am a blues guitarist known as Blind Lemon Blue. I've been blind since I was twelve, but I make great music. Mr. Galuf and I had a meeting. He drove me back to the club. When he dropped me off, I heard him back into another car. I'm sure he must have dented his car.
Mrs. Aydut:	My son Darren-Paul and I were walking past the Nexus Club when we heard this crash. We saw this old Lincoln back into a big trash container. I didn't see the dent, but the right fender must have been badly banged up.
D.P. Aydut:	I'm only eleven, but I know what I see. It happened just like my mother said. We saw this guy with a white cane and a guitar standing on the sidewalk. We ran up to Mr. Blind Lemon Blue and made sure that he was okay. When the Lincoln pulled away, I saw the dent in the trunk.
C.X. Kahn:	It's true that I was arrested a couple of years ago, but I've gone straight since then. This is the truth. When Mr. Galuf brought the car back, he slipped me $20 not to tell anyone about the dent.
J. Crebbs:	I don't like to air family dirty laundry in public, but my brother Milton runs a dishonest business. He always tries to cheat the public. He and I went our separate ways because he was always pulling scams like this.
E. Sheib:	I painted a blue Lincoln for Mr. Crebbs' Rent-A-Beaut and did a real nice job on it. We dropped it off at his lot on the morning of September 23. (Judge's note: That was the day that Mr. Galuf rented the car.)

Reflection Question: Which is fairer—the Jewish or the American rules of evidence? Why? What is fair and what is unfair about these rules of evidence?

MITZVAH OF THE WEEK: עֵדוּת COMING FORWARD TO TESTIFY

It is a mitzvah to give testimony before the Bet Din about all we know, whether a person will be sentenced through our testimony to death or to payment of goods and possessions, or whether someone will thus be spared goods, possessions or life. This is the meaning of Leviticus 5:1. In any matter of guilt or obligation we have a mitzvah to give testimony.

In civil cases—cases involving goods, money, and possessions—we need not come forward to testify. But if called, we must tell the truth. In criminal cases, in cases of the violation of Torah laws, we have an obligation to come forward and tell all we know whether or not we are called.

> In your opinion, what is the difference between testifying and being a tattletale? What is your responsibility toward each?

Aydut: Experience

Eli Wiesel teaches that today Jews need to be witnesses and speak up for justice. Brainstorm a list of five things that need a witness to speak up today.

Aydut: Resources

Here are some social justice websites that serve as witnesses.

Witness
http://www.witness.org/

The Innocence Project
http://www.innocenceproject.org/

Religious Action Center
http://www.rac.org/

Israel Religious Action Center
http://www.irac.org/

Add two more organizations to this list.

צו TZAV

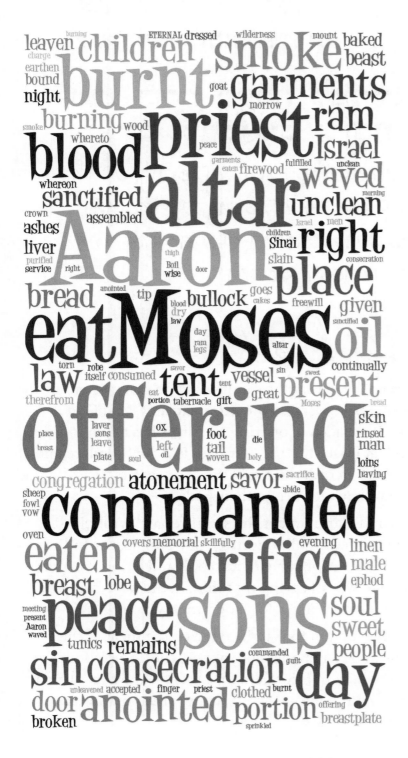

This portion describes
what the *Kohanim*
(priests) have to do in
the *Mishkan*. Then the
priests are taught how
to offer the sacrifices.
The Israelites are then
given the rules for
eating meat.

121

OUR TORAH TEXT: LEVITICUS 7:37

Leviticus is the book of the priests. We are now far enough into the book to establish that the *Kohanim* have their own mitzvot that affect all of Israel.

זֹאת הַתּוֹרָה לָעֹלָה לַמִּנְחָה וְלַחַטָּאת וְלָאָשָׁם וְלַמִּלּוּאִים וּלְזֶבַח הַשְּׁלָמִים.

זאת הורה לעלה למנחה לחטאת ולאשם ולמלואים ולזבח השלמים

This is the Torah of the burnt offering, of the meal offering, of the sin offering, of the guilt offering, of the consecration offering, of the sacrifice of the peace offering.

Exploring Our Torah Text

Maimonides believed that the sacrifices were given in order to wean the people of Israel away from idolatry, as if God were to say: "If the idea of offering sacrifices has taken too strong a hold, at least offer the sacrifices in a central place and observe the rules in order to avoid the excesses practiced by the idolaters when they sacrifice to their gods."

For Ibn Ezra and Nahmanides the sacrifices are symbolic. When a man offered a guilt-offering, for example, the killing of the animal and the offering of its blood and fat on the altar were a symbolic way of saying that this should have been the fate of the sinner were it not for God's mercy.

Why do you think that God commanded sacrifice?

A further reason taught for sacrifice is that the meat of the sacrifices was to be eaten in a holy place—the Temple for some sacrifices, anywhere in Jerusalem for others—and this turned the very act of eating into a sacred act by which man was brought nearer to God.

torah experience

We no longer offer daily sacrifices to God. Instead the daily prayers were developed as a way to connect with God on an individual level. The *Amidah* is considered our deepest prayer because in it we speak to God in praise, petition and thanks.

Use a Siddur to study the weekday *Amidah* with a partner. Then answer these questions.

On Shabbat, the middle thirteen blessings are removed. Why do you think that is?

If you were to write a personal *Amidah*, which blessings would you include and which would you change? What would you change them to, and why?

MITZVAH OF THE WEEK: תְּפִלַּת עֲמִידָה PRAYING THE AMIDAH

It is a positive commandment taught in the Torah that a Jew should pray every day. The origins of this are Exodus 23:25, "You shall serve the Eternal, Your God..." and Deuteronomy 11:13. Originally Jews fulfilled this mitzvah with sacrifices. Later these were replaced with the *Amidah*. How do you serve God with all your heart? The rabbis taught: Through prayer.

Ezra and his court arranged informal prayers into a formal practice, taking a practice that had been happening since the time of Moses and giving it an official structure.

Everyone would pray facing the Temple in Jerusalem.

They established eighteen benedictions (a nineteenth brakhah was added later).

Tifilat Amidah: Experience

Here are the middle blessings in the weekday *Amidah*. Create a pictorial chart that helps you remember them.

4.	*Binah*	We need wisdom.
5.	*T'shuvah*	We need repentence.
6.	*Slihah*	We need forgiveness.
7.	*G'ulah*	We need redemption.
8.	*Refu'ah*	We need healing.
9.	*Birkat ha-Shanim*	We need a year of blessings.
10.	*Kibbutz Galuyyot*	We need a return from exile.

continued on page 124

11. *Din* — We need justice.
12. *Birkat ha-Minim* — We need our enemies defeated.
(Some synagogues skip this.)
13. *Tzadikim* — We need righteous role models.
14. *Binyan Yerushalayim* — We need Jerusalem rebuilt.
15. *Malkhut Bet David* — We need the empire of David again.
16. *Shomei'a Tefillah* — We need our prayers heard.

Tifilat Amidah: Resources

The *Amidah* is the standing prayer. An "upstander" is someone who stands up for what is right and just. Here are some organizations that are upstanders.

Stand Up to Cancer
http://www.standup2cancer.org/

Stand Up for Excellence in Public Education
http://www.standup.org/

Stand Up for Kids
http://www.standupforkids.org/

BullyBust—Promoting a Community of Upstanders
http://www.schoolclimate.org/bullybust/upstander/resources

Google "upstander". What kind of sites do you find?

שמיני SHEMINI

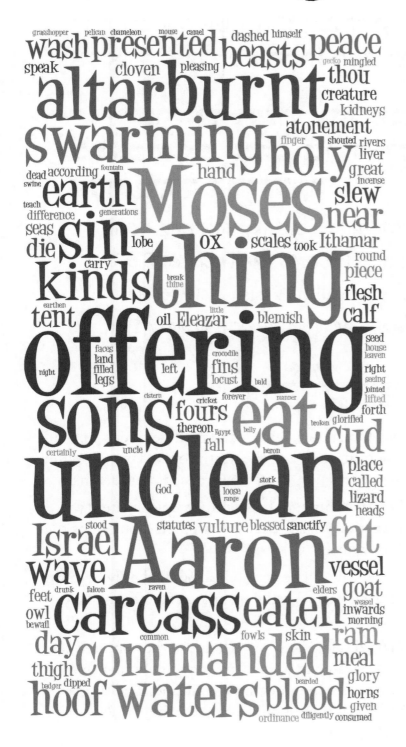

Overview: Leviticus 9:1–11:47

The *Mishkan* is dedicated, and the first sacrifices are offered. The sons of Aaron, Nadav and Avihu, die having offered a sacrifice with strange fire. Details for proper behavior of the priests follow this story, including that priests should not drink before doing priestly work. Rules of *kashrut*—which foods are permitted and which are forbidden—are given.

OUR TORAH TEXT: LEVITICUS 10:9

In this Torah portion Nadav and Avihu, two of Aaron's sons, *Kohanim*, are burned to death in an accident in the *Mishkan*. After than accident, Torah teaches this rule:

יַיִן וְשֵׁכָר אַל־תֵּשְׁתְּ אַתָּה וּבָנֶיךָ אִתָּךְ בְּבֹאֲכֶם
אֶל־אֹהֶל מוֹעֵד וְלֹא תָמֻתוּ חֻקַּת עוֹלָם לְדֹרֹתֵיכֶם.

יין ושכר אל תשת אתה ובניך אתך
בבאכם אל אהל מועד ולא תמתו
חקת עולם לדרתיכם

Wine and liquor don't drink, you and your children, when you come to the Tent of Meeting and you will not die: this is a permanent law, one for every generation.

Exploring Our Torah Text

Be a detective. Open up a *Tanakh* and read Leviticus 10:1–10. Write your own summary of the deaths of Nadav and Avihu. Give your own best guess as to what caused their deaths.

Rashi did the same thing. In his commentary he cites two possible explanations of the deaths (based on discussions the Rabbis held previously).

1. What evidence is there for the first explanation?
2. What evidence is there for the second explanation?
3. What do you think really happened?

Rabbi Eliezer said, "The sons of Aaron died only because they gave decisions on religious matters in the presence of their teacher, Moshe."

Rabbi Ishamel said, "They died because they entered the *Mishkan* intoxicated by wine. You may know that this is so because after their death God admonished those who arrived that they should not enter the *Mishkan* intoxicated by wine."

tORAH eXPerIeNCe

Bibliodrama of Leviticus 10:1–11

Questions to ask while students are in character:

Aaron: Why were you silent? What did you think of what your sons did?

Moses: Did you mourn your nephews? What did you think of what they did?

God: Why did you kill Nadav and Avihu? What did they do?

Mishael and Elzaphan: How did it feel to carry your cousin's sons outside of the camp? What were you thinking when you did this?

Moses: Why did you insist that Nadav and Avihu's family not mourn them?

Aaron, Eleazar, Ithamar: How did it feel to be forbidden to mourn your sons/ brothers? Did it change the way you served God?

Reflection Question: How does this story make you feel about your approach to being Jewish?

MITZVAH OF THE WEEK: יַיִן וְשֵׁכָר אַל־תֵּשְׁתְּ DON'T ABUSE ALCOHOL

If you look in *Sefer ha-Ḥinukh,* our verse generates this mitzvah for priests and for rabbis who are acting as judges:

> It is forbidden to enter the Temple or to give a legal verdict while drunk.

The Talmud *(Zevakhim 17)* explains,

> Intoxication produces three changes in a person: drowsiness, overconfidence, and a reduction of mental clarity. A *Kohein* must possess his full mental capacities when performing his service. A rabbi must have a perfectly clear mind before giving a verdict. Therefore, both are forbidden to drink before they do their sacred work.

In later commentaries we find:

> Nowadays, since our prayers have replaced sacrifices, and every Jew is responsible for the offerings of his or her heart, it is forbidden to pray while drunk. Drunken prayers are unacceptable and must be re-offered when sober *(Kreetot 13)*.

Don't Abuse Experience

These are the original Twelve Steps as published by Alcoholics Anonymous.

1. We admitted we were powerless over alcohol—that our lives had become unmanageable.

2. Came to believe that a Power greater than ourselves could restore us to sanity.

3. Made a decision to turn our will and our lives over to the care of God as we understood Him.

4. Made a searching and fearless moral inventory of ourselves.

5. Admitted to God, to ourselves, and to another human being the exact nature of our wrongs.

6. Were entirely ready to have God remove all these defects of character.

7. Humbly asked Him to remove our shortcomings.

8. Made a list of all persons we had harmed, and became willing to make amends to them all.

9. Made direct amends to such people wherever possible, except when to do so would injure them or others.

10. Continued to take personal inventory, and when we were wrong, promptly admitted it.

11. Sought through prayer and meditation to improve our conscious contact with God as we understood Him, praying only for knowledge of His will for us and the power to carry that out.

12. Having had a spiritual awakening as the result of these steps, we tried to carry this message to alcoholics, and to practice these principles in all our affairs.

Work with a partner. Decide which of the Twelve Steps would be the hardest.

Reflection Question: What is your addiction?

Don't Abuse Resources

There are several places that claim to connect Judaism to recovery from addiction. Here are two of the best.

Beit T'shuvah
http://www.beittshuvah.org/

JACs

http://www.jbfcs.org/programs-services/jewish-community-services-2/jacs/mission-statement-traditions

Find another interesting site on Judaism and addiction.

תזריע TAZRIA

This *parashah* and the next describe laws and procedures for impurity and skin diseases. Some things that can cause a person to be impure are childbirth, menstruation, contact with the dead, leprosy, etc.

129

OUR TORAH TEXT: LEVITICUS 13:45

In this *sidrah* and in the next we are given a lot of rules about leprosy. In Hebrew, *m'tzora* is the word for leprosy. Our verse gives the basics.

הַצָּרוּעַ אֲשֶׁר־בּוֹ הַנֶּגַע בְּגָדָיו יִהְיוּ פְרֻמִים
וְרֹאשׁוֹ יִהְיֶה פָרוּעַ וְעַל־שָׂפָם יַעְטֶה וְטָמֵא
טָמֵא יִקְרָא.

הַצָּרוּעַ אֲשֶׁר בּוֹ הַנֶּגַע בְּגָדִין יִהְיוּ
פְרֻמִים וְרֹאשׁוֹ יִהְיֶה פָרוּעַ וְעַל שָׂפָם
יַעְטֶה וְטָמֵא טָמֵא יִקְרָא

And a person who has the plague of leprosy shall have his clothes torn, his hair shaved, and he shall cover his upper lip and shall cry, "Unclean, unclean;" he shall live alone outside the camp.

Exploring Our Torah Text

In the Talmud and the Midrash the Rabbis ask, "Why does the Torah devote so much space to curing a skin disease?" They give several answers, including this one, which says that *m'tzora* is also a metaphor.

Rabbi Yoḥanan said in the name of Rabbi Yosi ben Zimra: "The spreading of *Lashon ha-Ra* (evil talk/ gossip) is equal to denying God."

He also said: "Whoever retells *Lashon ha-Ra* will be visited by plagues."

Resh Lakish said, "What is the real meaning of the verse, 'This is the Torah of *m'tzora*' (Leviticus 14:2)? It really means 'This is the Torah of one who is a *Motzi-Shem-Ra* (one who spreads gossip)'" (Arakhim 15b).

1. In the Talmud the Rabbis connect gossip and leprosy. How do they make this connection?

2. The Talmud says, "Why is gossip like a three-pronged tongue? Because it kills three people: the person who says it, the person who listens to it and the person about whom it is said" (Arakhin 15b). Explain this quote in your own words.

3. Have you ever experienced this quote in real life?

4. How did you deal with it?

5. Looking back, would you have done anything differently?

tORAH eXPeRIeNCe

Joseph Telushkin, in his book *Words that Hurt—Words that Heal: How to Choose Words Wisely and Well*, writes, "That words are powerful may seem obvious, but the fact is that most of us, most of the time, use them lightly. We choose our clothes more carefully than we choose our words, though what we say about and to others can define them indelibly. That is why ethical speech—speaking fairly of others, honestly about ourselves, and carefully to everyone is so important. If we keep the power of words in the foreground of our consciousness, we will handle them as carefully as we would a loaded gun."

Write a song or a rap about how words can get you in trouble.

Reflection Question: What are some words that have hurt you?

MITZVOT OF THE WEEK: מוֹצִיא שֵׁם רָע GOSSIP AND לָשׁוֹן הָרַע DEFAMATION OF CHARACTER

The Ḥafetz Ḥayyim explained the mitzvah of not speaking *Lashon ha-Ra* this way:

> You are forbidden to relate anything negative about others. If a negative statement is true, it is still considered to be *Lashon ha-Ra*. If it is false, even partly false, it is considered to be *Motzi-Shem-Ra* (defamation of character)—and is a much more severe offense. It cannot be repeated often enough that true negative statements are considered to be *Lashon ha-Ra*. The most common defense to a criticism for speaking *Lashon ha-Ra* is, "But it is true." That is exactly what categorizes the statement as being *Lashon ha-Ra*.

1. What is the difference between *Lashon ha-Ra* and *Motzi-Shem-Ra*?
2. Which is forbidden under Torah law?

Lashon ha-Ra Experience

Debate this case.

> Shira is running for class president against David. She starts a whisper campaign that says that David still wets his bed. David does still wet his bed, but that is a secret. In her speech Shira says, "You need a president who can get a good night's sleep." Everyone understands.
>
> David's family sues Shira for libel. They lose because David does wet his bed. Truth can't be libel.
>
> If the case was brought to a Jewish court, what do you think the court would say?

Lashon ha-Ra Resources

The ACLU is the free speech organization. It started as a Jewish organization.

ACLU
http://www.aclu.org/free-speech

Use the Internet to compare "free speech" and "responsible speech."

מְצֹרָע M'TZORA

Overview:
Leviticus
14:1—15:33

This *parashah* is the second round of dealing with leprosy. It talks about the priests' duties in curing leprosy, general procedures for curing leprosy and laws concerning house leprosy (diseases found in building stones). Laws concerning discharges from the body and the required acts of purification are also included.

OUR TORAH TEXT: LEVITICUS 14:9

In this passage we learn that once a leper is cleansed of *m'tzora*, immersion in water is the next step toward returning to society.

וְהָיָה בַיּוֹם הַשְּׁבִיעִי יְגַלַּח אֶת־כָּל־שְׂעָרוֹ
אֶת־רֹאשׁוֹ וְאֶת־זְקָנוֹ וְאֵת גַּבֹּת עֵינָיו וְאֶת־
כָּל־שְׂעָרוֹ יְגַלֵּחַ וְכִבֶּס אֶת־בְּגָדָיו וְרָחַץ
אֶת־בְּשָׂרוֹ בַּמַּיִם וְטָהֵר.

היה ביום השביעי יגלח את כל שערו
את ראשו ואת זקנו ואת גבת עיניו
ואת כל שערו יגלח וכבס את בגדיו
ורחץ את בשרו במים וטהר

On the seventh day the leper shall shave all hair off the head; any beard and eyebrows shall be shaved, clothing shall be washed, the leper's body shall be bathed in water, and so shall the leper be cleaned.

Exploring Our Torah Text

Here are five different events where dipping or washing is required.

In order to become pure after recovering from the skin disease, a leper must dip him/her self in a *mikvah* (a ritual bath of water).

In order to become pure and be ready to perform the holy work of the sacrifices, the *Kohein* must dip himself in a *mikvah*.

After his hands are clean, to become pure, a person must ritually wash them and say a *brakhah* before eating a meal.

In order to become pure and again to be permitted to her husband at the end of her menstrual period, a woman must dip herself in the *mikvah*.

In order to enact the final transformation, and as the ritual moment of change, a convert immerses him/her self in a *mikvah* and becomes a Jew.

What is the difference between "pure" and "clean"?

What do all five of these rituals have in common?

What seems to be the purpose of a *mikvah*?

torah experience

Visit a local *mikvah* or build a model *mikvah* or talk to people who either do *mikvah* regularly or have done it in the past.

Reflection Question: What is spiritually clean?

MITZVAH OF THE WEEK: מִקְוֶה MIKVAH

The tradition of the *mikvah* is one with roots in the Torah. The rabbis expound on the laws of the *mikvah*, explaining the physical requirements of the *mikvah* itself: It must be connected to a natural source of water and must have enough water to cover the body of an average person. There are many different reasons, traditional and modern, for going to a mikvah.

Mikvah Experience

Read the following passages.

> In brief, Jewish law requires husband and wife to refrain from any kind of physical contact during menstruation and for a period of seven days after its cessation. At the end of this period the woman, who is referred to as a *nidah*, or menstruant, bathes herself thoroughly and then immerses herself in a *mikvah* (literally, "a gathering of waters"). The *mikvah*, designed according to specific and ancient guidelines, is a specially constructed ritual pool with a natural water source. The wife recites the following blessing: "Blessed are You, O God, Ruler of the Cosmos, Who has sanctified us with *mitzvot* and has made it a *mitzvah* to observe the mitzvah of *t'vilah*, ritual immersion." Thereafter, husband and wife renew their physical relationship (Michael Kaufman, *Love, Marriage and Family in Jewish Law and Tradition*, Jason Aronson, 1992, page 195).

> Why then was I, a Reform rabbi and a committed feminist, splashing around in the *mikvah*? Was I going to make myself "kosher" for my new husband? Hardly. For me, it was an experience of reappropriation. The *mikvah* has been taken from me as a Jewish woman by sexist interpretations, by my experiences with Orthodox "family purity" committees who run communal *mikvaot* as Orthodox monopolies, by a history of male biases, fears of menstruation and superstitions. I was going to take back the water.

> To take back the water means to see *mikvah* as a wholly female experience: as Miriam's well gave water to the Israelites, so too will the *mikvah* give strength back to Jewish women. Water is the symbol of birth—now it can be a symbol of rebirth (Elyse M. Goldstein, "Take Back the Waters: A Feminist Re-Appropriation of *Mikvah*," *Lillith* no. 15, Summer 1986).

What meaning do you see in the mitzvah and ritual of *mikvah*?

(For the boys: Remember, men go to the *mikvah,* too, often just before Shabbat. Also *sofrim,* scribes, go to the *mikvah* before writing the name of God in a Torah scroll.)

Mitzvat Mayim Resources

The *mikvah* connects us to water. Not everyone in the world has easy access to clean and safe water. There are lots of organizations that are working on clean water. Here are a few.

Planet Water Foundation
http://www.planet-water.org/

Water Aid
http://www.wateraid.org/

Water for People
http://www.waterforpeople.org/

Project Wet
http://projectwet.org/

The Water Project
http://thewaterproject.org/

Find an interesting connection between "Israel" and "water".

אַחֲרֵי מוֹת AHAREI MOT

work offering send smoke day daughter
generations WASH assembly testimony midst astray
Egypt away vomited mother breeches household inhabitants
solemn home vomited mother sprinkle appointed woman
ordinances Moses come burnt house
iniquity statutes bathe garments
hands Aaron lifetime sacrifice son
beast bullock lot people priest
door meeting place veil
ark confess year bathe cut
father nations children anointed
hallow carnally ark father
die souls uncover law goat
cleanse holy death son near bullock come born alive burnt
tunic sin near blood goat
eat uncleannesses cover aunt
kill present afflict fowl Azazel uncleannesses profane men
water offering Israel
near altar place life sin lay fell lot
wife long camp coals
pour peace mitre leave clothes cover consecrated lamb
goat open beaten flesh attired
sacrifice rest door water bring
life everlasting Moses walk ox tent seed
drew kin tabernacle fat congregation east lewdness died
horns tent Israel land
ram born nakedness souls linen meeting
holy commanded stranger manner
things daughter God
round perversion present
small Aaron flesh clean
bring man sister doings
brother wilderness stranger camp seven
incense cloud begotten sweet
ETERNAL skins kinswomen

God gives more laws
and duties for the
Kohanim (priests),
including the
responsibilities of the
high priests on Yom
Kippur. Other laws about
fasting and atonement
on Yom Kippur are also
included. There are laws
about blood and eating
meat. The *parashah* ends
with the prohibitions
on inappropriate sexual
relations.

OUR TORAH TEXT: LEVITICUS 18:6

This *sidrah* contains a whole series of "Just say no" rules about sexual practices. It forbids incest and other acts, starting with this verse.

אִישׁ אִישׁ אֶל־כָּל־שְׁאֵר בְּשָׂרוֹ לֹא תִקְרְבוּ
לְגַלּוֹת עֶרְוָה אֲנִי יי.

אִישׁ אִישׁ אֶל כל שאר בשרו לא
תקרבו לגלות עֶרוה אֲני יי

None of you shall have sexual relationships with any person who is a close relative. Don't uncover their nakedness. I am the Eternal.

Exploring Our Torah Text: Leviticus 18:22

In this chapter we find this problematic verse.

וְאֶת־זָכָר לֹא תִשְׁכַּב מִשְׁכְּבֵי אִשָּׁה תּוֹעֵבָה הִוא

A man shall not lie with a man as with a woman.

REFORM: Clearly, the official arms of Reform Judaism have taken a most welcoming stance vis-à-vis lesbian and gay Jews who wish to learn, worship, give, live and love as Jews (Rabbi Don Rossoff, Temple B'nai Or, Morristown, NJ).

CONSERVATIVE: Conservative Judaism's Committee on Jewish Law and Standards, which until December 2006 held the same position as Orthodoxy, recently issued multiple opinions under its philosophy of pluralism, with one opinion continuing to follow the Orthodox position and another opinion substantially liberalizing its view of homosexual sex and relationships while continuing to regard certain sexual acts as prohibited.

RECONSTRUCTIONIST: The Reconstructionist movement, an American–born form of Judaism that grew out of the Conservative movement, has been a long-time supporter of both LGBT civil rights and the inclusion of LGBT people in Jewish life.

tOrAH experience

In Judaism there is a lot of talk about how to make each partner comfortable during sexual acts. For example, "When you are ready for sexual union, see that your wife's intentions combine with yours. Do not hurry to arouse her until she is receptive. Be calm, and as you enter the path of love and will, let her orgasm come first…" (The Holy Letter, attributed to Nachmanides)

Work in small groups to answer the following.

1. What are some responsibilities that lovers have?

2. In an intimate relationship, what are the most important things for people to work on to avoid causing pain to each other?

3. What are your personal obligations in bringing equality and mutuality to an intimate relationship?

Which of the following are important:

☐ Have each other's consent.

☐ Never use pressure to get consent.

☐ Be honest with each other.

☐ Treat each other as equals.

☐ Be attentive to each other's pleasure.

☐ Protect each other against physical and emotional harm.

☐ Guard against unintended pregnancy and STDs.

☐ Be clear with each other about what you want to do and don't want to do.

☐ Respect each other's limits.

☐ Accept responsibility for your actions.

[Note: These guidelines fit in with *v'ahavta l'rei-echa k'mocha* (love your neighbor as yourself) by striving to be respectful and helpful in our relationships.]

Using the above, have the students create a brochure that would be appropriate for Jewish middle and high school students.

Reflection Question: Are your fellow students well informed about sexual issues?

MITZVAH OF THE WEEK: לְגַלּוֹת עֶרְוָה UNCOVERING NAKEDNESS

Simply put, the mitzvot found in this passage ask you to establish and respect sexual boundaries. There are some sexual relationships that should not take place and some times when sexual relationships are not appropriate. The set of laws in this passage asks Jews to know and respect those boundaries. Today, for non–Orthodox Jews, defining and understanding these boundaries is not easy. It requires thinking and studying.

Two famous Jewish educators have said this about sex and Torah learning:

> We do not believe that sex in Judaism can be considered apart from love, from personhood, from the ideal of holiness. To turn sex education into basic biology is to debase it from a Jewish point of view. Biological data is important, but only as a means. The end is a loving human being whose sexuality is expressed with another in a way that makes them both holier—that is, closer to God—than they were before (Rabbi Eugene and Estelle Borowitz).

Ariyot Experience

To follow the Borowitzes' example, look at the following list from Michael Gold's *Does God Belong in the Bedroom?*

1. Luann, a high school senior, has a boyfriend who says, "If you love me, you will sleep with me."

2. Jack and Jill decided to live together before marriage to see if they are really compatible.

3. A public high school wants to establish a clinic that will provide birth control for students.

4. Sally is sexually abused by her stepfather, who tells her not to tell anyone.

5. Fred discovers that his wife, Sheila, has carried on an extramarital affair.

6. Barry decides to remain a virgin until marriage although other boys make fun of him.

7. Janet, fifteen years old, is pregnant after sleeping with her boyfriend.

8. Steve and Judy tell the rabbi before their wedding that they plan not to have children.

9. Rhonda, married with a child, wants to leave her husband for a lesbian lover.

10. George's parents have told him that masturbation is a sin that leads to disease.

11. A pornographic theater opens in a Jewish neighborhood.

12. A youth group is having an overnight trip and wants boys and girls to sleep in the same room.

13. Bob and Laurie, married ten years with no children, decide to have a baby using in vitro fertilization (Michael Gold, *Does God Belong in the Bedroom?* JPS, 1992).

Discuss these situations in class. And if you want to learn more, you can get either Rabbi Gold's or Rabbi Friedman's book.

Reflection Question: What makes sex so difficult to talk about?

Ariyot Resources

The "nakedness" was a form of protection for woman and children who were abused. Today a lot of organizations protect women and children from abuse.

Stop Child Trafficking Now
http://www.sctnow.org/

Project Meridian Foundation
http://www.projectmeridianfoundation.org

National Network to End Domestic Violence
http://www.nnedv.org

Child Abuse Prevention Association
http://childabuseprevention.org/

Find an organization that helps Jewish families.

קְדוֹשִׁים KEDOSHIM

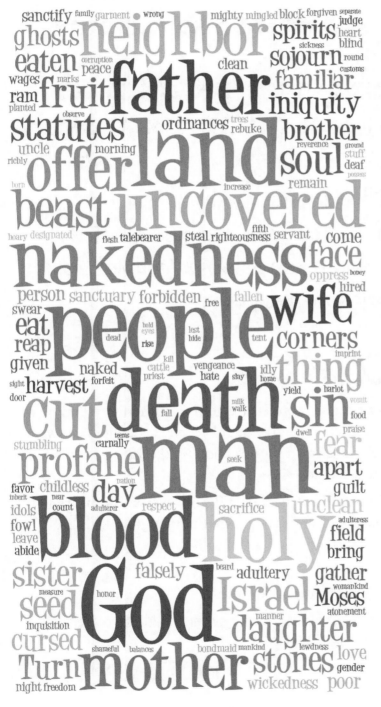

Overview:
Leviticus
19:1—20:27

The *parashah* includes the Holiness code, which is a series of laws that include respecting parents, not worshipping idols, observing Shabbat, eating sacrifices right away, leaving the corners of fields, not stealing, not taking advantage of handicaps, judging cases fairly and not hating people. Perhaps the most famous line in the code: "Love your neighbor as yourself."

OUR TORAH TEXT: LEVITICUS 19:17

In the verse right after our verse, we are told you should love your neighbor as yourself. Our verse is about doing something that at first doesn't seem like love.

לֹא־תִשְׂנָא אֶת־אָחִיךָ בִּלְבָבֶךָ הוֹכֵחַ תּוֹכִיחַ
אֶת־עֲמִיתֶךָ וְלֹא־תִשָּׂא עָלָיו חֵטְא.

לא תשנא את אחיך בלבבך הוכח
תוכיח את עמיתך ולא תשא עליו
חטא

You shall not hate your neighbor in your heart; you must tell your neighbor what is wrong about his or her behavior and not do a sin because of your neighbor.

Exploring Our Torah Text

The mitzvah here is rebuke. It is telling someone when he or she is doing something wrong. *Tokhehah* is the Hebrew word for rebuke. Read this quotation about *tokhehah* and answer the following questions.

> One who rebukes another will in the end find more favor than one who flatters that person (Proverbs 28:23).

Questions

Explain this verse in your own words.

Why would one who gives *tokhehah* "find more favor" than one who gives flattery?

Have you ever experienced this verse to be true? When?

torah experience

Maimonides adds:

> *Tokhe<u>h</u>ah* cannot be given in a way that publicly embarrasses or shames the one you are trying to help (Maimonides, Laws of Character, 6.7).

> What are a few guidelines that Maimonides might provide on how to give rebuke?

Make a list in two columns. The first list should be "Successful and Worthy Rebukes" and the second list should be "Unsuccessful and Unworthy Rebukes".

Reflection Question: When has criticism helped you?

MITZVAH OF THE WEEK: הוֹכֵחַ תּוֹכִיחַ אֶת־עֲמִיתֶךָ REBUKE YOUR FRIEND

It is a mitzvah to rebuke a fellow Jew who does not behave properly in matters between people and God or between people. The proper way of reproving someone is to do it privately, in a soft tone, and with gentle, sincere words, so that the person will not be shamed.

If the alleged sinner does not accept private reproval, one may correct the person in the presence of close friends and relatives. Should this, too, prove unsuccessful, it is permissible to publicly admonish the person, even though it may be humiliating.

> If you see a person doing wrong and the sinner will not accept your words, then you are exempt from this mitzvah. For the Rabbis of the Talmud teach us, "Just as it is a mitzvah to say something that will be heeded, so is it a mitzvah not to say what will not be heeded" (*Yevamot* 65b) (*Sefer ha-<u>H</u>inukh*).

Tokhe<u>h</u>ah Experience

Our friend Mark Borovitz brought us this problem:

> Sam is twelve years old. He and Davis, a "good bud," are at the school playground, hanging. No one else is around. Davis starts talking about breaking into the school and messing up the science lab to get even with the teacher, who is "a piece of work." Sam hates the teacher, too. He also knows that breaking and entering and vandalizing are against the law,

and he is afraid that they might get caught. He tells Davis, "I don't think that this is a good idea. We're gonna get busted." Davis calls him a wimp.

How should Sam respond?

Your Responsa

Obviously Sam should not break into the school and destroy someone else's property. We will not insult you with that question. These other questions are also important.

What should Sam say to Davis?

If Davis decides to break in on his own, should Sam go to the police?

If the police suspect Davis and question Sam, what should Sam do?

Reflection Question: Who would you like to give *tokhehah,* and what would you like to say?

Tokhehah Resources

Tokhehah is what the prophets did. It is a voice screaming "What you are doing is wrong!" In today's world a number of organizations act like prophets crying out to try to confront and stop the evil in the world. By and large, the prophets were not liked, especially not by the people they criticized. Not all of these organizations are liked, but they try hard to speak up for justice.

Amnesty International
http://www.amnesty.org/

B'Tselem
http://www.btselem.org/

Wikileaks
http://wikileaks.org/

Jewish World Watch
http://www.jewishworldwatch.org/

Find another website that speaks up for others who need a voice.

אמר EMOR

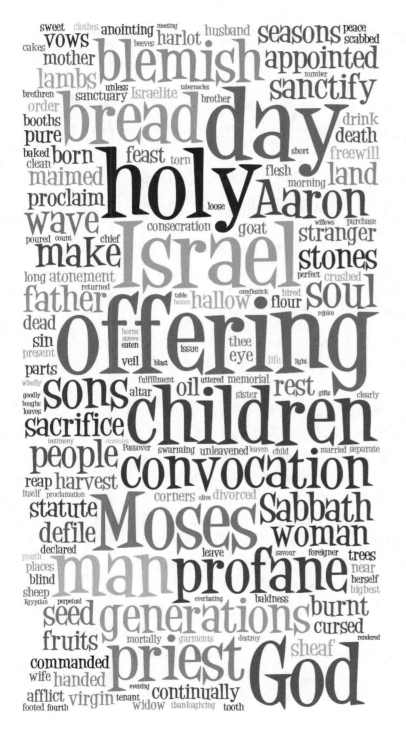

Overview: Leviticus 21:1–24:23

This portion includes even more rules about the *Kohanim* (priests), including rules about the priests coming in contact with the dead, and about serving as a priest. Rules about celebrating Shabbat, Passover, the Omer, Shavuot, Rosh ha-Shanah, Yom Kippur and Sukkot are described. There is a story about a man who cursed God.

OUR TORAH TEXT: LEVITICUS 22:32

From our verse we learn two important mitzvot about God's public image—the state of God's name.

וְלֹא תְחַלְּלוּ אֶת־שֵׁם קָדְשִׁי וְנִקְדַּשְׁתִּי
בְּתוֹךְ בְּנֵי יִשְׂרָאֵל אֲנִי יי מְקַדִּשְׁכֶם.

ולא תחללו את שם קדשי ונקדשתי
בתוך בני ישראל אני יי מקדשכם

Do not profane My Holy Name, rather I will be made holy among the Families-of-Israel.

Exploring Our Torah Text

From this verse and a couple of others, the Rabbis suggest that we can make God's name holy, and we can dishonor God's name, too.

The assertion that people, with all their limitations and faults, can hallow God, and that God requires people to hallow the Divine Name, is known in rabbinic literature as *Kiddush ha-Shem*. People are sanctified by God if they choose to follow the mitzvot, thus imitating God's ways. It is likewise the duty of people to hallow God. "I will be hallowed among the Families-of-Israel; I am The Eternal who hallows you" proclaims the Torah.

Kiddush Ha-Shem and its opposite, <u>Hillul ha-Shem</u> (profanation of God's name) became one of the basic polarities of Judaism. The Jew was required to look upon himself as a guardian of her or his people's reputation. Any extraordinary act that would bring honor to the Jewish people was regarded as *Kiddush Ha-Shem*.

One of the best-known examples of *Kiddush ha-Shem* that the Talmud relates concerns an incident in the life of Shimon ben Shetah, who found a valuable gem hanging around the neck of a camel he had bought from an Arab. His disciples urged him to keep the treasure that God had bestowed upon him. However, Shimon quickly returned the stone, saying, "I purchased an animal, not a precious stone."

When the Arab was given back the stone, he exclaimed, "Blessed be the God of Shimon ben Shetah; blessed be the God of Israel." Here God's name became hallowed because Shimon demonstrated that his belief in God was real, so real that he did not succumb to the temptation of taking advantage of an innocent person. He caused a non–Jew (prior to Islam) to praise the God of Israel. (*The Language of Judaism*, Simon Glustrom, Ktav Publishing House, Inc. [1973]).

What can we do to make God's name holy?

What can we do to dishonor God's name?

torAH eXPerIeNce

Work with a group of students and act out a situation that shows a time when a person either did *Kiddush ha-Shem* or *Hillul ha-Shem*. Perform your piece without explanation. Have the rest of the class explain which it was and why.

Reflection Question: Is the idea that your actions reflect on God a useful idea or not?

MITZVAH OF THE WEEK: חִלּוּל הַשֵּׁם HILLUL HA-SHEM AND קִדּוּשׁ הַשֵּׁם KIDDUSH HA-SHEM

Applying Our Mitzvah

Glueckel of Hamelin (1646–1724) is one of the most interesting characters in German Jewish history. Despite the fact that she was a successful businesswoman, she found time to rear and to marry off twelve of her thirteen children, allying them with the most notable Jewish families of Europe.

During the years 1691–1719 Glueckel, who had moved from Hamelin to Hamburg, wrote her memoirs in Judaeo-German. This work of hers is a most unusual one, for autobiography is rare in Jewish literature in this age, and as a medium of self-expression by a woman of this period it is altogether unique.

The Thief Who Died a Martyr, about 1670

At that time an East Indian ship with many uncut diamonds fell into the hands of the King of Denmark and lay at Gluckstadt. There were two Jews there who knew that a citizen in Norway had a large batch of these diamonds. They took evil counsel together, regrettably, and formed a partnership to get the diamonds out of the house where they were kept.

So these two—this bad lot—came to Norway. At once they made a careful search for the man who had the diamonds and managed to get into his home. Gradually they became so friendly with this man that they found out where he kept his treasures, got the best of him, and took everything away from him. The man had sheltered them in his home. The next morning they left the house and rented a skiff and thought they had made a good job of it all. But the Almighty did not want this to succeed. When the man arose the next morning and asked about his two guests, the servant told him that they had left the house quite early. The man was rather disturbed, for whoever has such a treasure is always worried. Therefore he went to the chest where he kept his treasures but found nothing. He immediately took it for   granted that his two guests had done this to him. He ran straight for the sea and asked some boatmen if they had not seen two Jews pulling out. "Yes," said one of them to him, "such-and-such a boatman took them away about an hour ago." He hired a boat immediately, put in four oarsmen, and started after them. It was not very long before they sighted the boat with the thieves, but when the thieves saw that

150

they were being followed they threw the whole treasure into the sea.

In short, the man overtook them, and they had to go back with him. They denied everything while they were being stripped naked and everything was being carefully searched. But all this did not help them. They were put to such severe torture that finally they had to confess that they had done it, and both were condemned to the gallows.

The one thief immediately accepted the Christian faith (and saved his life). The other had been a pious man all his life with a pious father and mother. He came from Wandsbeck (on the outskirts of Hamburg). He did not want to change his religion and chose to sacrifice his life. I knew him and his parents well, and all his life he had behaved himself as a pious, honest man. He must have been led astray by the other fellow, who was never any good, and so it was inevitable, unfortunately, that he should come to a bad end. Surely his soul is in Paradise, for he must have actually attained future life through his conduct in his last hour. He could have escaped just as easily as his companion, but he fulfilled the commandment (Deuteronomy 6:5): "Thou shalt love the Lord thy God with all thy soul (even though you die a martyr to prove your love of God)."

Did this second man perform *Kiddush ha-Shem* and, as Glueckel suggests, die a martyr? Explain your opinion.

Kiddush ha-Shem/Hillul ha-Shem Experience

Take five cards. Make a list of five things that you can do to make God proud. Go into small groups. Pool your cards. Make a shared list of your to ten things (out of all the cards) that will make God proud. Share your lists with the class.

Reflection Question: Do you believe that your actions affect God's feeling?

Kiddush ha-Shem/Hillul ha-Shem Resources

People are created in the image of God. That means that every time we do something that makes God proud, we are living up to our ideal image. Every time we do something that embarrasses God, we are behaving poorly. Here are some organizations that live up to the best we can do. All of them make healing possible.

Direct Relief
http://www.directrelief.org/

Project C.U.R.E.
http://www.projectcure.org/

Doctors Without Borders
http://www.doctorswithoutborders.org/

The K.I.N.D. Fund
http://www.nbcnews.com/id/40558738/

Find the URL of another project that would help you express being created in God's image.

בְּהַר BE-HAR

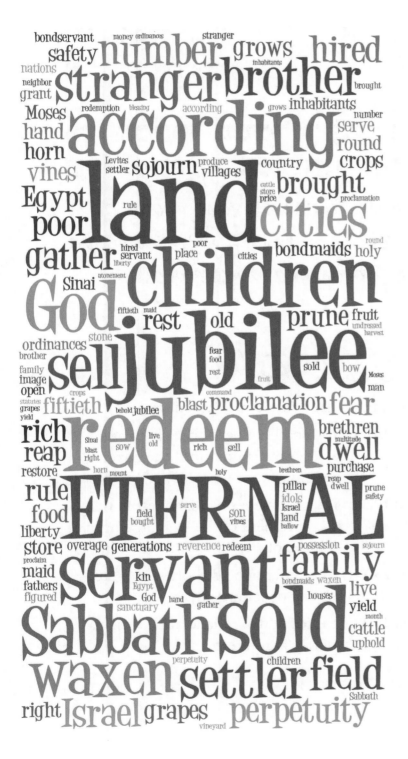

bondservant money ordinances stranger
safety number grows hired
nations inhabitants brother
neighbor stranger brought
grant redemption blessing according grows inhabitants number
Moses according serve
hand Levites round
horn settler sojourn produce villages country crops
vines land store brought
Egypt rule cattle price proclamation
poor cities
gather hired poor bondmaids holy round
Sinai servant place cities
God children prune fruit
fiftieth maid rest old undressed harvest
ordinances stone jubilee sold bow
brother fear food Moses
family sell rest fruit man
image crops command
open statutes behold jubilee blast proclamation fear
grapes fiftieth jubilee
yield rich redeem rich sell brethren
reap Sinai live dwell
blast sow old multitude
restore right holy purchase
rule horn mount brethren reap dwell
food ETERNAL pillar prune
liberty field idols safety
store bought serve son Israel
overage generations reverence redeem land hallow
proclaim servant family possession sojourn
maid kin bondmaids waxen live
fathers Egypt hand gather houses yield
figured sanctuary sold month
Sabbath cattle uphold
waxen perpetuity settler field Sabbath
right Israel grapes perpetuity
vineyard

Overview: Leviticus 25:1–26:2

More rules! (And you thought your parents had a lot of rules for you!) This portion includes rules for the Sabbatical years, Jubilee years, owning property in the land of Israel, and not lending money at interest.

153

OUR TORAH TEXT: LEVITCUS 25:14

While we have seen little bits of this idea before, our verse of the week shows us that business is not separate from religion, but rather that the mitzvot specifically cover business practice.

וְכִי־תִמְכְּרוּ מִמְכָּר לַעֲמִיתֶךָ אוֹ קָנֹה מִיַּד עֲמִיתֶךָ אַל־תּוֹנוּ אֶת־אָחִיו.

וכי תמכרו ממכר לעמיתך או קנה מיד עמיתך אל ותנו את אזיו

If you sell some to one of your people or buy something from the hand of your people, do not cheat a person who is your brother.

Exploring Our Torah Text

In the Torah there are a lot of business mitzvot.

Leviticus 19:13: You shall not keep the wages of a worker overnight until the next morning.

Leviticus 19:35: You shall never be dishonest in the measurement of the weight, length or volume of anything you are selling.

Leviticus 25:14: You shall not be dishonest in either buying or selling anything.

Leviticus 25:37: It is forbidden to lend a fellow Jew money at interest.

What do these laws teach?

tOrAH eXPerIeNce

Consider this <u>H</u>asidic story.

Reb Zusia was a very poor man all his life. When his wife's dress became worn out and she was in need of a new one, he borrowed some money from a few friends, bought the needed material and handed it to his wife to give to the tailor. A few weeks later Reb Zusia asked his wife whether the tailor had finished the garment. With a sigh she replied, "He finished the dress, but I don't have it." "What happened?" Reb Zusia asked in surprise. She began to explain, "When the tailor's future son-in-law saw him sewing a dress, he assumed that it was surely for his bride (the tailor's daughter).

"But when he learned that it was not, the young man became angry, and the tailor began to worry lest the engagement be jeopardized. So I immediately gave the dress to the girl as a present."

At this point in the story Reb Zusia became concerned that a business mitzvah was being violated. Can you guess which one? What advice do you think he gave his wife?

_____

_____

_____

_____

_____

_____

_____

_____

"And how much did you pay the tailor?" asked Rev Zusia. "For what?" asked his wife. "For making the dress," he replied. "Why on earth should I pay him for making the dress when it ended up being for his own daughter?" Reb. Zusia stated firmly, "How could you even consider withholding the man's wages? The whole week long he has been working for you and not for his daughter. He has been waiting anxiously to finish this job so that he will be able to receive his payment in order to sustain his family. What is the poor man going to do now? Is it his fault that you decided to give the dress to his daughter?" Hearing these words, Reb Zusia's wife set out immediately to borrow some money and paid the tailor his wages.

What is the moral of this story?

Write your own <u>H</u>asidic story that teaches the importance of one of the other three business mitzvot.

Reflection Question: What does religion have to do with business?

MITZVAH OF THE WEEK: גְּנֵבַת דַּעַת MISREPRESENTATION

The *Shul<u>h</u>an Arukh*, in dealing with the laws of theft, first legislates against blatant fraud:

One is forbidden to beautify the article being sold in order to create a false impression. So one is forbidden to dye a slave's hair or beard in order to make him appear young. One is not allowed to give an animal bran to eat that makes her hair brown and upright, thus creating the impression that she is fat and sleek. Nor may one comb her artfully in order to create the same impression. One is not allowed to paint old baskets to make them look new, nor is one allowed to soak meat in water to make it look fatty.

Example I: Mixing good and bad quality: A vendor who has a mixture of good- and not-so-good–quality merchandise must not place the good quality on top so as to create the impression that the whole lot is of good quality.

Example II: Second-class goods sold as first-class: Second-class goods with minor faults or of inferior quality (not noticeable to the customer) must not be sold as first-class goods.

Example III: Faults in new or second-hand goods: A mechanical object that was returned because it was not working to perfection must not be sold to another person without pointing out the fault (for example, electrical goods or clocks with even a minor fault).

Example IV: False claims: One must not say to a customer, "You will be getting an exceptional bargain" if in reality one is charging the normal price.

Example V: Overcharging: A buyer who offers a high price for an object that is not so valuable (an antique, a piece of jewelry or a rare postage stamp) must be told by the vendor what the current price is.

Example VI: Under-paying: If a vendor is not aware of the high value of the goods he is offering for sale (a rare antique, a painting or old *seforim*) and he is asking for a low figure, the buyer must offer the true market price of the goods (*A Torah Guide to the Businessman*. Rabbi S. Wagschal, Feldheim Publishers, 5757-1990).

Al Tanu Experience

Work in a group. Take five cards (or pieces of paper). Write down a situation on each piece of paper. Some cases should be examples of ways business should not be done. Some of these cases should be examples of the way that business should be done. Don't say which is which. Switch your cards with another group. Judge those cases as to good or bad business practices. Meet with the other team and go over the results.

Reflection Question: This verse says "your people." Do you think this applies to everyone or to just a specific group?

Al Tanu Resource

There are lots of Jewish business ethics sites because it is a big Jewish topic. Here is one of the not-for-profit organizations.

Jewish Accociation for Business Ethics
http://www.jabe.org/

Find three articles on Jewish business ethics that you can understand.

בחקתי BE-HUKKOTAI

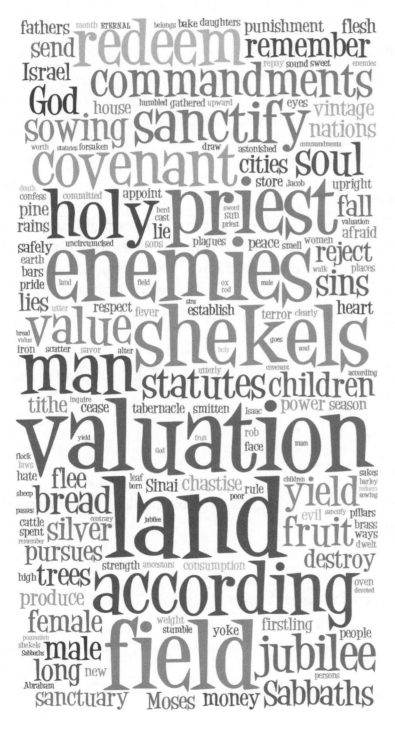

Overview: Leviticus 26:3–27:34

God promises five blessings to the Families-of-Israel if they follow the laws prescribed in the Torah. Then God warns of thirty-two curses that will happen if the laws are not followed. And in case we hadn't received enough laws, the book of Leviticus ends with laws about vows, tithes, things promised to God and things that need to be redeemed.

OUR TORAH TEXT: LEVITICUS 27:2

In this *sidrah* is a verse where we learn about a very important Jewish legal category, the oath. For Jews, the words "I swear to God" have very important and powerful ramifications.

דַּבֵּר אֶל־בְּנֵי יִשְׂרָאֵל וְאָמַרְתָּ אֲלֵהֶם אִישׁ
כִּי יַפְלִא נֶדֶר בְּעֶרְכְּךָ נְפָשֹׁת לַיָי.

דבר אל בני ישראל ואמרת אליהם
איש כי יפלא נדר בערכך נפשת ליי

Speak to the Families-of-Israel and tell them:
"When a person clearly says a vow to the
Eternal, you have to evaluate it."

Exploring Our Torah Text

Our teacher, Dr. Stephen Passamaneck, translated this responsum case into English.

> A man, Feibush of Munich, swore a false oath before Jewish tax assessors in Regensburg, lying about his taxable income. Having been caught, he now stands repentantly before us, the local Bet Din. What should be done with him? (Jacob Bazak, *Jewish Law and Iewish Life*, UAHC 1979, Translated and Edited by Stephen M. Passamaneck)

What would you recommend that the Bet Din do?

torah experience

Study these texts with a partner. Pick the one that you think is most important.

> A person taking an oath must be worthy, and there must be no suspicion of falsehood, either intentional or unintentional, in an oath. For that reason the Rabbis almost completely abolished oaths from court procedure and substituted other regulations *(Shulḥan Arukh, Ḥoshen Mishpat,* Laws of Judges 12.2).

> The punishment for taking a false oath is very severe, since it involves the desecrating of God's name (Adin Steinsaltz, *The Talmud: A Reference Guide*).

> You shall not tell a lie; The Eternal will not clear anyone who swears falsely by God's name (Exodus 20:7, the Ten Commandments).

> If a person intentionally gives false evidence about a neighbor, you should do to that person exactly what was planned for the neighbor. Thus you will sweep out evil from your community—others will hear and be afraid, and such evil things will not come again in your community (Deuteronomy 19:18–20).

Reflection Question: How would the world change if everyone was honest about oaths?

MITZVAH OF THE WEEK: נֶדֶר TAKING AN OATH

In the Bible and in the Talmud, taking an oath was a very serious action. It was something that Jews didn't want to do unless it was absolutely necessary. Even if people thought they were telling the truth in an oath, a mistake could cause them to swear falsely by God's name. These texts above will help you understand that an oath was a very serious matter (Hillel Gamoran, *The Jewish Law Review Vol. 2*).

How does the mitzvah of honesty in oaths fit into your life?

Neder Experience

Here is the actual *t'shuvah* that Rabbi Jacob ben Judah Weil wrote on the case of Feibush of Munich (page 159).

Answer: We read in Talmud *(Shevu'ot 39a)*: The entire world trembled when God on Sinai uttered the prohibition, "Thou shalt not take the Name of the Eternal your God in vain" *(Exod. 20:7)*. The Rabbis designated a false oath as one of the most serious transgressions. R. Elazar of Worms wrote in his collection, the *Roke'ah*, no. 25, that a false oath is the same as denying the existence of God. Therefore I say this: Feibush of Munich shall be flogged three (ceremonial) lashes just prior to the *v'Hu Rahum* portion of the evening worship service. This is to take place in the synagogue on three occasions, a Monday, a Thursday and the next following Monday (weekdays that are distinguished by a public reading of Torah and more worshippers). After the lashes he is to declaim in a voice clearly audible to all, in the German language, "I have sworn falsely on my tax declaration! I have sinned; I have done iniquity; I have acted illegally." Moreover, once Feibush's sin became public knowledge, it constituted a public desecration of God, which is not to be treated lightly.

The *Roke'ah* further provides that the malefactor "shall be flogged several times and shall fast for forty consecutive days, except upon Sabbaths and other religious holidays. When the forty-day period is over, he shall continue to fast for a number of days equal to the number of Sabbaths that fell during the original forty-day period. Thereafter he shall fast on Mondays and Thursdays for one full year. If he is physically incapable of sustaining the fast after the forty-day period, he shall give money to public charity and undertake another personal deprivation prescribed by the religious authorities of his city. He shall forever refrain from making any sort of oath—even on a matter which is manifestly true..." (Jacob Bazak, *Jewish Law and Jewish Life*, UAHC 1979, translated and edited by Stephen M. Passamaneck).

Is this a fair verdict and sentence? Why?

Reflection Question: Where in society do we need honesty?

161

Neder Resources

Here are some foundations whose work centers on honesty.

The Center for Food Integrity
http://www.foodintegrity.org/

The Chopra Foundation
http://www.choprafoundation.org

Values.com
http://www.baldfacedtruth.org/

Find a website that teaches something interesting about truth. Share the interesting thing.

בְּמִדְבַּר BE-MIDBAR

Overview: Numbers 1:1—4:20

The fourth book of the Torah opens with a census. The community counts men over the age of 20, primarily so the Families-of-Israel can determine who can defend them. Instructions are given for where each tribe should camp. Aaron's family is listed, and other clans are identified.

163

OUR TORAH TEXT: NUMBERS 3:1-2

In this *sidrah* an innocent line listing the names of the sons of Aaron teaches us a powerful lesson about the act of teaching.

וְאֵלֶּה תּוֹלְדֹת אַהֲרֹן וּמֹשֶׁה
בְּיוֹם דִּבֶּר יְיָ אֶת־מֹשֶׁה בְּהַר סִינָי.
וְאֵלֶּה שְׁמוֹת בְּנֵי־אַהֲרֹן הַבְּכוֹר נָדָב
וַאֲבִיהוּא אֶלְעָזָר וְאִיתָמָר.

וְאלֶה תולדת אהרן ומשה ביום דבר
יי את משה בהר סני ואלה שמות בני
אהרן הבכור נדב ואביהוא ואלעזר
ואיתמר

These are the descendants of Aaron and Moses on the day that the Eternal spoke with Moses at Mount Sinai. And these are the names of the sons of Aaron: Nadav, the first born, Avihu, Eleazar and Itamar.

Exploring Our Torah Text

To understand the power of this verse, we need to also read Rashi:

> Why does the Torah state that Aaron's sons, Nadav, Avihu, Elazar and Itamar, were the sons of both Aaron and Moses, when in fact only Aaron was their biological father?
>
> The Torah also credited Moses in order to teach us that one who teaches a child Torah is credited as if he or she had brought the child into the world
>
> (*Sanhedrin* 19b).

Explain this commentary's lesson in your own words.

tORAH eXPeRIeNCe

Write a few sentences about the best Jewish teacher you've ever had. (And because it would embarrass him or her, your present teacher doesn't count.)

Make a gift for the teacher you wrote about. It could be
- Poem
- Micrography of selected Jewish texts
- card with Jewish values as to why the teacher is so important to you

MITZVAH OF THE WEEK: וְשִׁנַּנְתָּם לְבָנֶיךָ AND YOU SHALL TEACH THEM DILIGENTLY

This mitzvah applies to every person, old and young, rich and poor alike. Every person must set aside a specific time to study Torah each day. Included in this mitzvah is the obligation of every parent to teach his or her children Torah. A parent should begin to educate a child in Torah as soon as the child begins to speak, by teaching the child the verse "Moshe commanded us the Torah; it is a heritage of the congregation of Ya'akov" (Deuteronomy 33:4). And when the child reaches the age of five the parent should begin teaching the child Torah.

V'Shinantam Experience

Interview a class teacher or synagogue educator about
why he or she became a teacher/educator.

V'Shinantam Resources

The Torah asks Israel to start counting men for soldiers at the age of twenty. No
age is good for soldiers, but twenty isn't bad. Today many children are forced into
armies. These sites work to keep children from having to go to war.

Child Soldiers International
http://www.child-soldiers.org/

Amnesty International
http://www.amnestyusa.org/our-work/issues/
children-s-rights/child-soldiers

Human Rights Watch
http://www.hrw.org/topic/childrens-rights/child-
soldiers

Make a list of places where child soldiers are still being used.

נָשֹׂא NASO

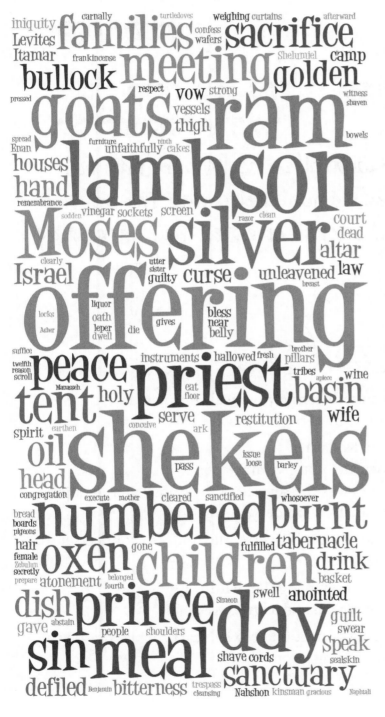

iniquity · carnally · turtledoves · weighing · curtains · afterward
Levites · families · confess · sacrifice · camp
Itamar · frankincense · meeting · Shelumiel · golden
bullock · respect · vow · strong · witness · shaven
pressed · goats · vessels · ram · thigh · bowels
spread · furniture · ninth · cakes
Enan · unfaithfully
houses · lamb · son
hand · razor · clean
remembrance · sodden · vinegar · sockets · screen · court · dead
Moses · silver · altar
clearly · utter · unleavened · law
Israel · guilty · curse · breast
locks · liquor · bless
oath · gives · near
Asher · leper · die · belly
dwell
suffice · peace · instruments · hallowed · fresh · brother
twelfth · reason · priest · pillars · wine
scroll · Manasseh · holy · eat · tribes · apiece · basin
tent · floor · wife
spirit · earthen · serve · restitution
conceive · ark
oil · shekels · issue · barley
head · pass · loose
congregation · execute · mother · cleared · sanctified · whosoever
bread · numbered · burnt
boards
pigeons
hair · oxen · gone · fulfilled · tabernacle · drink
female · Zebulun · secretly · children · basket
prepare · atonement · belonged · fourth
dish · prince · swell · anointed
gave · abstain · day · guilt
people · shoulders · swear
sin · meal · Simeon · Speak
shave · cords · sealskin
sanctuary
defiled · Benjamin · bitterness · trespass · Nahshon · kinsman · gracious · Naphtali
cleansing

Overview: Numbers 4:21–7:89

More rules for the *Kohanim* (priests), the suspected adulteress (*Sota*), and the *Nazir* (one who makes a vow). The tribe of Levi is assigned to move the *Mishkan*. The *Kohanim* are taught the words of *Birkat Kohanim* (which is now included in the blessing of the children on *Erev Shabbat*). The chieftains bring gifts. Moses talks to God in the Tent of Meeting.

167

OUR TORAH TEXT: NUMBERS 7:9

In this *parashah* we learn something of the *Kohanim*'s special relationship with the *Mishkan* and the Ark of the Covenant.

וְלִבְנֵי קְהָת לֹא נָתָן כִּי־עֲבֹדַת הַקֹּדֶשׁ עֲלֵהֶם
בַּכָּתֵף יִשָּׂאוּ.

לבני קהת לא נתן כי עבדת הקדש
עלהם בכתף ישאו

But to the Kohathites he [Moses] did not give any [oxen], since theirs was the service of the (most) sacred objects, they carried by shoulder.

Exploring Our Torah Text

An early twentieth century biblical commentator, the S'fat Emet, explains our verse this way:

> But to the Kohatites
> he [Moses] did not give any [oxen],
> since theirs was the service of the (most) sacred objects,
> they carried by shoulder. (Numbers 7:9)

To make sense out of this verse, the midrash connects it to another verse.

> Raise up a song, bang the drum
> add a sweet harp and a lyre. (Psalms 81:3)

But what is the connection between carrying things on the shoulder and singing a song?

168

This can only be understood by looking at the Hebrew. In First Samuel we have the story of David bringing the ark to Jerusalem that has a verse which reads:

And the cows went straight along the way. (1 Samuel 6:12)

The Hebrew word וַיִּשַּׁרְנָה *Va-yiSHARnah* is used for straight.

The Zohar explains this verse this way: "Because they were carrying the ark to Jerusalem they were granted the ability to sing (שָׁרוּ *sharu*)." The Zohar reads: "It was the Ark on their backs that enabled them to sing."

The same is true of the Levites (including the family of the Kohathites) who carried the ark on their shoulders and were giveN the power to lift their voices in song.

This is also true of every person who serves God. True service fills a person with light and joy.

1. What is our verse?
2. What other verse is used to explain our verse?
3. According to the Zohar, "What happened to the cows that carried the ark?"
4. How does the S'fat Emet (using the Zohar) explain why the family of Kohat had to carry the ark personally and were given no oxen to do the job?
5. How does this lesson apply to every Jew?

torah experience

"But to the Kohathites he [Moses] did not give any [oxen], since theirs was the service of the (most) sacred objects, they carried by shoulder." (Numbers 7:9)

What did it feel like to carry the Mishkan?

Practice carrying the biggest Torah in the sanctuary "on your shoulders" with a partner. The class will help spot you.

How did it feel?
What must the feeling have been to carry the Mishkan through the desert?

MITZVAH OF THE WEEK: וּנְשֹׂאַת אֲרוֹן הַקֹּדֶשׁ CARRYING THE ARK

It was mitzvah for the *Kohanim* to carry *Aron ha-Kodesh* (the Holy Ark) on their shoulders whenever the need arose for it to be transported from one place to another. Most authorities agree that the entire tribe of Levi was permitted to carry the Holy Ark; in other words, both Kohanim and Levi'im. It was forbidden to transport the Holy Ark in a wagon (coach) or on the back of an animal *(Sefer ha-Hinukh)*.

Mitzvah Experience

It ain't heavy, it's my Torah!

> The first ark for the Ten Commandments was built while the Families of Israel were wandering in the desert. It was made of acacia wood covered with gold. A midrash says it was so heavy that it took the strength of many men even to budge it. But then, the midrash explained, once they lifted it, it carried its carriers.

> David Moshe of Thortkov was a Ḥasidic rabbi. Once during the dedication of a new Sefer Torah he had to lift a large, heavy scroll for a long time. One of his students offered to help him, but he said, "Once you've picked it up, it is no longer heavy."

We no longer have an ark of the covenant. We cannot in our day and age literally perform this mitzvah. Make a metaphor out of it. How would you explain today''s meaning of carrying the ark on your shoulders, not in a wagon?

What do you do to fulfill this mitzvah?

Mitzvah Resources

If you Google "Torah Rescue" you may find a scandal about a *sofer* who made allegedly false claims about Holocaust Torah scrolls. Here is a link to a place that really rescued Torah scrolls from the Holocaust.

 Czech Memorial Scroll Trust
http://www.czechmemorialscrollstrust.org/

Find out what a new Sefer Torah costs. Find out what it costs to receive a Holocaust Torah.

בְּהַעֲלֹתְךָ BE-HA'ALOTEKHA

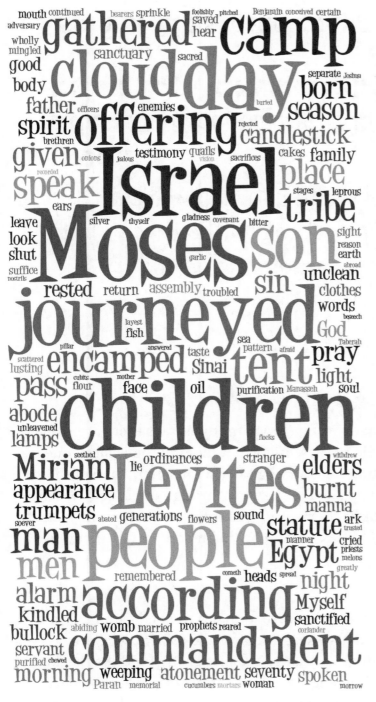

**Overview:
Numbers
8:1–12:16**

The menorah is described. The Levites become assistants to the Priests. The first celebration of Passover in the desert is described and followed by the second Passover for those who were unclean at the time of the first. God's signs, the cloud and the fire, lead the people during the day and at night. The Families of Israel complain again about food, and a fire breaks out. The council of seventy elders is established. Moses marries a Cushite woman; Aaron and Miriam complain about this. Miriam gets leprosy. Moses prays to God to heal her.

171

OUR TORAH TEXT: NUMBERS 9:11

This is the *parashah* that introduces many of the mitzvot of Passover. Read our verse and figure out the seder practices it describes.

בַּחֹדֶשׁ הַשֵּׁנִי בְּאַרְבָּעָה עָשָׂר יוֹם בֵּין הָעַרְבַּיִם יַעֲשׂוּ אֹתוֹ עַל־מַצּוֹת וּמְרֹרִים יֹאכְלֻהוּ׃

בחדש השני בארבעה עשר יום בין הערבים יעשו אתו על מצות ומררים יאכלהו

In the second month on the fourteenth day at dusk, they shall eat it (the Paschal lamb) with matzah and maror.

What specific parts of the seder come from this verse?

Exploring Our Torah Text

Pesa<u>h</u> has many mitzvot. Maimonides says there are eight altogether. Six of these involve removing the *hametz*; one involves eating matzah (together with *maror*). One of them involves telling the Pesa<u>h</u> story (through the seder). We are going to look at the meaning of three terms: *hametz*, *matzah* and *maror*. This lesson will be much easier to do if you use a Haggadah.

Hametz

These two meditations are found in the Haggadah. One of them is read before searching for the *hametz*. The other is read before burning the *hametz*. *Hametz* is any food that is bloated or that has risen because of the effects of yeast. Jews declare anything that is made from grain and has not been inspected and declared *kosher l'Pesah* to be *hametz*. Before Passover it is traditional to collect and burn *hametz*. (Some Jews make collecting *hametz* a chance to donate food to non–Jewish charities.)

Searching for Hametz

What is the connection between *hametz* and the evil inclination?

May it be Your will, God, that we merit to search our souls for the blemishes that we foolishly placed in it by following the evil inclination's advice, and that we merit true repentance. Please, God, in Your mercy and for Your honor, help us to be protected from the prohibition of *hametz*, even from a crumb, this year and every year, for as long as we live. Amen, may it be Your will.

Burning the Hametz

Based on these meditations, what lesson can be learned from the searching out, removing and burning of *hametz*?

May it be Your will, God, that just as I have removed the *hametz* from my house and properties, so, too, should You remove all the forces of evil, and the spirit of evil shall be removed from the earth. May our evil inclination be removed from us and may you grant us a pure heart. May all the forces of the Other Side and wickedness vanish like smoke and the kingdom of the wicked be eradicated. May You destroy all those that challenge the Divine Presence with vengeance and judgment, just as You destroyed the Egyptians and their idols in those days at this season, Amen.

Use a Haggadah to help answer these questions.

Matzah

1. Define matzah.
2. What do you think is the meaning of eating matzah?

Maror

1. What is maror?
2. What is the meaning of maror?

torah experience

Run a mock seder in the classroom focusing on the items on the seder plate and the ritual/explanation surrounding them.

MITZVAH OF THE WEEK: מְעוֹת חִטִּים MA'OT HITTIM

In the Haggadah recited at the seder we declare: "All who are hungry, let them come and eat." Our nation experiences freedom ourselves and must ensure that our brothers and sisters have the means to celebrate freedom, too.

In reality, however, as we begin our seder most of the people who are hungry will not be standing in our dining rooms, waiting for the invitation. So in preparation for the Passover holiday, it is an age-old Jewish tradition to contribute generously to funds that ensure that everyone who is in need has the necessary provisions for the holiday—food, matzah, wine, festive clothing, etc.

This special Passover fund, originally intended to provide the poor with matzah, is known as *ma'ot hittim*, the "wheat fund".

Ma'ot Hittim Experience

In a small group make a shopping list for a Passover seder for four. Your teacher will help you to know what foods can and can't be purchased for Passover. This will vary from synagogue movement to synagogue movement. Then research (online or at an actual market) the cost of your list. How much does it cost to make Passover?

Ma'ot Hittim Resources

Ma'ot Chitim
http://www.maotchitim.org/

Amit Children
http://amitchildren.org/how-you-can-help/
maot-chittim/

Ma'ot Hittim is more of a local thing than a national or international one. Find a local organization that does Ma'ot Hittim.

שְׁלַח-לְךָ SHELAH-LEKHA

Under the leadership of Joshua and Caleb, twelve spies are sent to the Land of Israel. They return with a detailed report but give a recommendation to not enter the land. Only Joshua and Caleb push to conquer the land. The Families-of-Israel become afraid and rebel. God threatens to wipe out the Families-of-Israel but relents when Moses intercedes. God then decides that all Israelites who escaped from Egypt will not enter the Land of Israel. The laws of *tzitzit* conclude this *parashah*.

175

OUR TORAH TEXT: NUMBERS 15:38

In this *sidrah* we meet the third paragraph of the *Shema*. It has a new mitzvah to teach us.

דַּבֵּר אֶל־בְּנֵי יִשְׂרָאֵל וְאָמַרְתָּ אֲלֵהֶם
וְעָשׂוּ לָהֶם צִיצִת עַל־כַּנְפֵי בִגְדֵיהֶם לְדֹרֹתָם
וְנָתְנוּ עַל־צִיצִת הַכָּנָף פְּתִיל תְּכֵלֶת.

דבר אל בני ישראל ואמרת אלהם
ועשו להם ציצת על כנפי בגדיהם
לדרתם ונתנו על ציצת הכנף פתיל
תכלת

Speak to the Families-of-Israel and tell them,
"Throughout your generations make fringes
on the corners of your clothes, and to put in
each fringe a thread of blue."

Exploring Our Torah Text

The tallit is a four-cornered garment with fringes on each of the four corners. Each of the fringes is called a *tzitzit* and must consist of an exact formula of five knots and thirty-nine wrappings.

The next two verses explain the purpose of *tzitzit*.

> It will be your *tzitzit*, when you look at it, you will remember all the mitzvot of the Eternal, and do them, so that you will not go whoring after your own eyes and your own heart, after which you are led astray. That you will remember and do all My mitzvot, and be holy to your God.

How do the *tzitzit* remind you of the mitzvot?

EXPERIENCING THE TORAH

Get each student four pieces of string. Three pieces should each be about a yard long. One should be about a yard. Find a YouTube video on how to tie *tzitzitziot*. Use your string to practice the knots.

Reflection Question: We know what the knots are supposed to mean. What do they mean to you?

MITZVAH OF THE WEEK: צִיצִית TZITZIT

How do the *tzitzitziot* help to remind Jews of the responsibility of the mitzvot? How does looking at them help to urge us to do mitzvot?

Fact
248 = number of bones in the human body
248 = number of positive (Thou Shalt) mitzvot
365 = number of days in a year
365 = number of negative (Thou Shalt Not) mitzvot
613 = total number of mitzvot

Fact

א	Alef	1	ז	Zayin	7	מ	Mem	40	צ	Tzade	90
ב	Bet	2	ח	Het	8	נ	Nun	50	ק	Kuf	100
ג	Gimmel	3	ט	Tet	9	ס	Sameh	60	ר	Resh	200
ד	Dalet	4	י	Yud	10	ע	Ayin	70	ש	Shin	300
ה	Heh	5	כ	Kaf	20	פ	Peh	80	ת	Tav	400
ו	Vav	6	ל	Lamed	30						

Add up the value of the letters in **צִיצִית** *tzitzit*.

צ   Tzade   = _____

י   Yud   = _____

צ   Tzade   = _____

י   Yud   = _____

ת   Tav   = _____

                           value of the word *tzitzit*
+ 8   =   number of strings in a *tzitzit*
+ 5   =   number of double knots in a *tzitzit*
_____

_____ total

What sorts of things would wearing *tzitzit* remind you to do?

Tzitzit Experience

Make your own tallit. This may be a good project to do with your parents.

Check out Make Your Own Tallit Project

http://www.torahaura.com/item_Tallit_20x70_With_Atarah_White.aspx

Also look at the Duct Tape Tallit:

http://tapbb.wordpress.com/2012/02/09/the-duct-tape-tallit-yes-you-can/

Reflection Question: What does it feel like to wear a tallit?

Tzitzit Resources

Make your own tallit—Torah Aura Productions
www.torahaura.com

My Jewish Learning
http://www.myjewishlearning.com/life/Life_Events/
BarBat_Mitzvah/Practical_Aspects/Planning_Guide/
Personalizing_Through_Art.shtml

Go on a tallit hunt. Find a tallit you would like to buy on the internet.

קֹרַח KORAH

KORAH

Overview: Numbers 16:1–18:32

Korah and his followers (250 chieftains) rebel against Moses and Aaron. God ends the rebellion and threatens to destroy everyone. This time Moses and Aaron intercede, and only the rebels are punished. We learn of more laws: duties of the *Kohanim* (priests) and Levites, laws of the firstborn that should go to the priests and laws of tithing.

OUR TORAH TEXT: NUMBERS 18:24

A tithe is ten percent. In this *parashah* we have a mitzvah that has to do with tithing.

כִּי אֶת־מַעְשַׂר בְּנֵי־יִשְׂרָאֵל אֲשֶׁר יָרִימוּ לַיי תְּרוּמָה
נָתַתִּי לַלְוִיִּם לְנַחֲלָה...

כי את מעשר בני ישראל אשר ירימו
ליי תרומה נתתי ללוים לנחלה

Redeem a tenth of the fields of the Families-of-Israel as a gift I have given to the Levites.

Exploring Our Torah Text

Use a piece of paper with a grid of squares ten across by ten down as your field. As you read each of these rules, mark off the portions of the field that must be taken as tithes.

The word *ma'aser* means a tenth. To understand how it impacts the idea of tzedakah we need to look at the rules for Jewish farmers. While there are all kinds of rules—rules about vineyards, rules about orchards, rules about herds and so on—we are only going to look at the rules on fields.

Ma'aser

> ONE TENTH OF EVERYTHING THAT GROWS IN THE LAND, WHETHER IT IS GRAIN THAT HAS GROWN IN THE GROUND OR FRUIT THAT HAS GROWN ON A TREE, MUST BE SET APART AND GIVEN TO THE ETERNAL (Leviticus 27:30).

This means giving it to the tribe of Levi for the work they do in running the worship in the tent of meeting (Numbers 18:21). Mark the *ma'aser* on your field by coloring in a tenth of your crop (ten squares).

181

Ma'aser Sheni

> TAKE A TENTH OF THE CROP THAT REMAINS AFTER THE
> MA'ASER AND EAT IT BEFORE THE ETERNAL YOUR GOD IN
> THE PLACE THAT IS CHOSEN FOR THE DIVINE DWELLING
> PLACE (the Tabernacle and later the Temple)
> (Deuteronomy 14:23).

Ma'aser Sheni means the second tithe (tenth). There are ninety squares left in your field after *ma'aser*. We need to mark one tenth of the ninety. Mark the *ma'aser sheni* on your field by marking nine more squares.

Ma'aser oni means the poor tithe (tenth). Every third year the Torah tells us to take the second tenth (after the *ma'aser* has already been taken) and use it as a gift to the poor instead of a personal pilgrimage food. Because we've already marked these squares, don't mark anything.

Pe'ah

> AND WHEN YOU REAP THE HARVEST OF YOUR FIELDS,
> YOU SHALL NOT TOTALLY HARVEST THE FIELD. YOU MUST
> LEAVE THE CORNERS OF THE FIELD...FOR THE POOR AND
> THE STRANGER (Leviticus 23:22).

Pe'ah means corner. This mitzvah orders farmers to leave the corners of their fields (at least one sixtieth) for people in need. This allows poor people to come and do the work to harvest their own food without having to ask for tzedakah. To indicate *pe'ah,* mark and color two squares of your field.

Shikhehah

> WHEN YOU REAP THE HARVEST OF YOUR FIELD AND YOU
> FORGET A SHEAF IN THE FIELD, DO NOT GO BACK TO GET
> IT. LEAVE IT FOR THE STRANGER, THE FATHERLESS AND
> THE WIDOW (Deuteronomy 24:19).

Shikhehah means forgotten. This a mitzvah for which you can't plan. You can't plan to forget something. You also cant ever know how much youll forget. For the sake of this exercise, mark two more squares for *shikhehah*.

Leket

> AND WHEN YOU REAP THE HARVEST OF YOUR FIELDS...
> YOU SHALL NOT GATHER THE GLEANINGS OF YOUR
> HARVEST (Leviticus 19:9).

Leket means gleanings. Gleanings are things that the people harvesting dropped or didn't bother to pick. As with *shikhehah*, you can't plan the amount of gleanings that will be left. For this exercise, mark two squares of *leket*.

Pe'ah, shikhehah and leket are all gifts to the poor that allow the poor to work for their own food without having to beg or ask for help.

> How much should be given to tzedakah? If the person can afford it, as much as is needed by the poor. But if the person cannot afford that much, the person should give up to twenty percent of what he or she has. That is the highest degree of tzedakah. Ten percent is considered average, and less than that is considered cheap (*Yoreh De'ah 249.1*).

Based on the texts you've studied on farming, where do you think the rabbis came up with these figures?

Reflection Question: Why do you think the rabbis set two limits on giving—one for how much one could give and another for how little one should give?

MITZVAH OF THE WEEK: מַעֲשֵׂר MA'ASER

Allocations is a big word, one that has to do with money. Collecting tzedakah is only part of the job. It is a big responsibility, but the other responsibility is in deciding how the money will be allocated. The big problem with tzedakah is that the need is bigger than the resources, so someone is forced to make the choice of which good work to fund. Working on allocations is not an easy or fun responsibility, but it is an important one.

Experiencing Ma'aser

Use this exercise to help in your allocation process of your tzedakah money.

Part I—The Amount of Money

- The amount of tzedakah money we have to distribute is $ _____
- With one dollar I could buy myself _____
- With five dollars I could buy myself _____
- With twenty dollars I could buy myself _____
- If I had all of our tzedakah money to spend on me, I would buy myself _____

  _____

- A mitzvah that could be accomplished with one dollar is _____
- A mitzvah that could be accomplished with five dollars is _____
- A mitzvah that could be accomplished with twenty dollars is _____
- A mitzvah that could be accomplished with a hundred dollars is _____

Part II—Our Past History of Giving

What do we know about where our tzedakah money went last year?

PLACE	KIND OF WORK	AMOUNT

Part III—Planning For This Year

What sort of rules or standards should we set for the people or places that receive tzedakah from us?

1) _____

2) _____

3) _____

Based on these standards, what questions do we want to ask about each recipient?

1)_____

2)_____

3)_____

4)_____

5)_____

Use a blank sheet of paper to decide where you want your tzedakah money to go to this year.

Ma'aser Resources

Here are ten different tzedakah organizations. Some are Jewish. Some are secular.

 Heifer International
http://www.heifer.org/

Jewish Free Loan Society
http://www.freeloan.org/

 Dorot
http://www.dorotusa.org/

The Giraffe Heroes Project
http://www.giraffe.org/

 Feeding America
http://feedingamerica.org/

Have different groups research different organizations and make reports to your class. Can you pick one for a tzedakah project? Can you add to this list?

חקת HUKKAT

Overview: Numbers 19:1–22:1

There are still more laws to teach—laws of the red heifer and rituals and laws of purification. Miriam and Aaron die. The people complain again about water. God instructs Moses to talk to the rock, and instead he strikes it. Water pours forth. The king of Edom refuses to let the Families-of-Israel pass through his land. The Families-of-Israel fight battles with the Canaanites, Amorites and Og, king of Bashan.

OUR TORAH TEXT: NUMBERS 20:11

In this week's *sidrah* Moses commits the sin that keeps him from entering the land of Israel. Here it is.

וַיָּ֤רֶם מֹשֶׁה֙ אֶת־יָד֔וֹ וַיַּ֧ךְ אֶת־הַסֶּ֛לַע בְּמַטֵּ֖הוּ פַּעֲמָ֑יִם וַיֵּצְא֤וּ מַ֙יִם֙ רַבִּ֔ים וַתֵּ֥שְׁתְּ הָעֵדָ֖ה וּבְעִירָֽם ׃

וירם משה את ידו ויך את הסלע במטהו פעמים ויצאו מים ריבם ותשת העדה ובעירם

Moses lifted up his hand and hit the rock with his staff twice, and much water went out, and the congregation drank, and so did their cattle.

Exploring Our Torah Text

When the commentators read this story carefully, they wound up disagreeing on Moses crime. They came up with a number of different possibilities.

Maimonides: His sin was that he got angry and insulted the people rather than being patient and working with them.

Nahmanides: His sin was comparing himself to God by saying, "Shall we bring forth water for you?" rather than giving God all the credit.

Albo: His sin was lack of faith. He did not believe that God's command to talk to the rock would be enough to effect the miracle.

Rashi: He failed to reinforce the people's faith, because the miracle would have been greater if he had followed God's command and only spoken to the rock.

Read the entire story in Numbers 20 and decide which of these four interpretations you like, or if you can find a better one. Explain your thinking.

torah experience

Have a debate. Resolved: Moses was a good leader.

MITZVAH OF THE WEEK: לֹא תְבַיֵּשׁ DO NOT EMBARRASS

"Therefore, one must take great care not to do anything which may cause shame to anyone in the world. This also applies to Torah study. If in the course of discussion you hear your friend err, you should not tell the friend, 'You have erred' or 'You don't understand what you are saying,' or the like, so that the friend will not be ashamed. But you should say to the friend, 'I received it thus from my teacher,' or you should give the impression of not having heard the error" (*Orhot Tzaddikim: The Ways of the Righteous*).

How do we embarrass others?

What can we do to avoid embarrassing others in what we do and say?

Expereincing Al Tivayesh: Stopping Bullying

Role-play the following situation.

[1] For the first time ever, Jackie's mother gives her a credit card and lets her go shopping for a new school outfit on her own. Jackie comes home with an outfit that her mother hates. Her mother thinks that it is ugly, inappropriate for school, and doesn't make Jackie look good. The outfit does not play to Jackie's strengths. Jackie walks in all excited, goes upstairs and puts on the outfit, and comes down the steps like a model. She asks her mother, "Isn't this just wonderful? Isn't it the best?" How should her mother answer? What should she say?

[2] Max and Julian are out on the playground during recess. Julian isn't feeling happy and wants to be alone. Max is not great at reading people. He

never knows what to say and usually says too much. Max keeps starting conversations with Julian. Julian ignores him, but Max doesn't get it. Because Julian is the only one not playing ball, Max wants to talk to him. Julian does not want anyone to know that he is working on a problem, but he wants Max to go away. What should he say?

[3] Zane and his cousin Danielle go to the mall together. They see Jordan, a kid from Zane's school, who Danielle thinks is really cute. Zane knows that Jordan gets in a lot of trouble. He thinks that Danielle should not try to get to know him. What should Zane tell her?

Resources: Bullying

Bullying is the most extreme form of embarrassing. Here are some websites that work against bullying.

It Gets Better Project
http://www.itgetsbetter.org/

Stop Bullying—U.S. Dept. of Health & Human Services
http://www.stopbullying.gov/

PACER's National Bullying Prevention Center
http://www.pacer.org/bullying

Find out how many LGBT youth kill themselves each year due to bullying.

בָּלָק BALAK

Overview: Numbers 22:2–25:9

On the journey the Families-of-Israel meet the nation of Moav. Balak, the king, hires Balaam, the seer, to curse the Families-of-Israel. Instead of cursing them, Balaam blesses the people in the famous story of Balaam and his donkey. Balaam prophesies that the foes of the Families-of-Israel will be conquered. The Israelites take part in sacrifices to Ba'al Peor.

190

OUR TORAH TEXT: NUMBERS 22:6

In this *sidrah* we have the story of Balaam and his famous talking animal. Here is a foreign prophet who ultimately gives Israel a famous blessing.

...כִּי יָדַעְתִּי אֵת אֲשֶׁר-תְּבָרֵךְ מְבֹרָךְ
וַאֲשֶׁר תָּאֹר יוּאָר.

כי ידעתי את אשר תברך מברך
ואשר תאר יואר

For I know that whomever you bless is blessed and whoever you curse is cursed.

Exploring Our Torah Text

It is a mitzvah to not listen to a false prophet or a fortune-teller. In this day and age cults are one of the closest things we have to false prophets.

In the Talmud the rabbis claim that Balaam is a false prophet, a soothsayer. It is a commandment to not listen to a false prophet. There is also a mitzvah to kill false prophets. The rabbis therefore wonder why God allows a false prophet to give an important blessing.

To understand this question, we need to learn about false prophets. Here is a lesson from Joel's childhood rabbi, Beryl D. Cohan.

> These prophets roamed the country the way gypsies do. There were many of them. The Bible speaks of "a company of prophets." This is true of all the false prophets: They moved about in large groups. The true prophets were lonely men who lived and thought very much alone...

191

The true prophets never engaged in much emotionalism; they spent time in meditation and prayer, pretty much in solitude. Heavy burdens rested on their hearts... These raving, chanting, dancing prophets were foretelling the future—foretelling the future the way gypsy fortune-tellers do—and were paid for their services.

The true prophets never received pay for their speaking...Many people consult fortune-tellers; it is a foolish practice, but nevertheless, many do. Some people do it for the fun of it; others are more serious about it. How does a fortune-teller know what will happen? She (usually it is a woman) will gaze into a crystal ball, or read the palms of the questioner's hands….

We shall hear them (real prophets) say, over and over again: "It shall come to pass," and, "thus said the Lord," predicting that this or that would happen if the people and their kings and priests persisted in their bad ways.

What are some other groups that trap people through involvement?

Rabbi Cohan's answer doesn't directly answer the question. What do you think he was trying to teach about false prophets?

TORAH EXPERIENCE

Watch "The Simpsons" cult episode (Season 9, episode 13, "The Joy of Sect") and discuss. It is on Hulu, among other places.

MITZVAH OF THE WEEK: NOT LISTENING TO A FALSE PROPHET

In his book of Jewish law, the *Mishneh Torah*, Maimonides expands this section into fifty interrelated mitzvot about false prophets and idolatry.

Read this list. Put an **E** in front of all the mitzvot that are easy for you to accept. Put an **H** in front of all the mitzvot that are hard for you to accept. Put a **?** in front of all those you have a hard time understanding. Discuss the list with your class.

_____ 24. Not to inquire into idolatry (Lev. 19:4)

_____ 25. Not to follow the whims of your heart or what your eyes see (Num. 15:39)

_____ 26. Not to blaspheme (Ex. 22:27)

_____ 27. Not to worship idols in the manner in which they are worshipped (Ex. 20:5)

_____ 28. Not to worship idols (in the four ways we worship God) (Ex. 20:5)

_____ 29. Not to make an idol for yourself (Ex. 20:4)

_____ 30. Not to make an idol for others (Lev. 19:4)

_____ 31. Not to make (human) forms even for decorative purposes (Ex. 20:20)

_____ 32. Not to turn a city to idolatry (Ex. 23:13)

_____ 33. To burn a city that has turned to idol worship (Deut. 13:17)

_____ 34. Not to rebuild it (as a city) (Deut. 13:17)

_____ 35. Not to derive benefit from it (Deut. 13:18)

_____ 36. Not to missionize an individual to idol worship (Deut. 13:12)

_____ 37. Not to love the missionary (Deut. 13:9)

_____ 38. Not to cease hating him (Deut. 13:9)

_____ 39. Not to save him (Deut. 13:9)

_____ 40. Not to say anything in his defense (Deut. 13:9)

_____ 41. Not to refrain from incriminating him (Deut. 13:9)

_____ 42. Not to prophesize in the name of idolatry (Deut. 18:20)

_____ 43. Not to listen to a false prophet (Deut. 13:4)

_____ 44. Not to prophesize falsely (in the name of God) (Deut. 18:20)

_____ 45. Not to be afraid of killing the false prophet (Deut. 18:22)

_____ 46. Not to swear in the name of an idol (Ex.23:13)

_____ 47. Not to perform *ov* (the work of a medium) (Lev. 19:31)

_____ 48. Not to perform *yid'oni* (the work of a magical seer) (Lev. 19:31)

_____ 49. Not to pass (your children through the fire) to Molekh (Lev. 18:21)

_____ 50. Not to erect a column (as a public place of worship) (Deut. 16:22)

_____ 51. Not to bow down on smooth stone (Lev. 26:1)

_____ 52. Not to plant a tree (in the Temple courtyard) (Deut. 16:21)

_____ 53. To destroy idols and their accessories (Deut. 12:2)

_____ 54. Not to derive benefit from idols and their accessories (Deut. 7:26)

_____ 55. Not to derive benefit from ornaments and idols (Deut. 7:25)

_____ 56. Not to make a covenant with idolaters (Deut. 7:2)

_____ 57. Not to show favor to them (Deut. 7:2)

_____ 58. Not to let them dwell in our land (Ex. 23:33)

_____ 59. Not to imitate them in customs and clothing (Lev. 20:23)

_____ 60. Not to be superstitious (Lev. 19:26)

_____ 61. Not to go into a trance (to foresee events, etc.) (Deut. 18:10)

_____ 62. Not to engage in astrology (Lev. 19:26)

_____ 63. Not to mutter incantations (Deut. 18:11)

_____ 64. Not to attempt to contact the dead (Deut. 18:11)

_____ 65. Not to consult the *ov* (Deut. 18:11)

_____ 66. Not to consult the *yid'oni* (Deut. 18:11)

_____ 67. Not to perform acts of magic (Deut. 18:10)

_____ 68. Men must not shave the hair off the sides of their head (Lev. 19:27)

_____ 69. Men must not shave their beards (with a razor) (Lev. 19:27)

_____ 70. Men must not wear women's clothing (Deut. 22:5)

_____ 71. Women must not wear men's clothing (Deut. 22:5)

_____ 72. Not to tattoo the skin (Lev. 19:28)

_____ 73. Not to tear the skin (in mourning) (Deut. 14:1)

_____ 74. Not to make a bald spot (in mourning) (Deut. 14:1)

Experiencing Navi Sheker

Here is the way the Torah describes a false prophet.

> If a prophet, or one who foretells by dreams, appears among you and announces to you a miraculous sign or wonder, and if the sign or wonder of which he has spoken takes place, and he says, "Let us follow other gods" (gods you have not known) "and let us worship them," you must not listen to the words of that prophet or dreamer. The Eternal your God is testing you to find out whether you love God with all your heart and with all your soul. It is the Eternal your God you must follow, and God you must love. Keep God's mitzvot and obey God; serve God and hold fast to God. That prophet or dreamer must be put to death, because he preached rebellion against the Eternal your God, who brought you out of Egypt and redeemed you from the land of slavery; God has tried to turn you from the way the Eternal your God commanded you to follow. You must purge the evil from among you
> (Deut. 13:1–5).

Film a TV commercial for a false prophet.

Navi Sheker Resources

Cults are a form of false prophets. The problem is that all religions start out as cults. Some cults are dangerous and some are not. Below is a website that lists and talks about cults. Have your class research and create a list of dangerous cults.

Watchman Fellowship
http://www.watchman.org/

Imagine someone in your family became a member of a cult. Find someone you would trust to rescue your family member. Also, find an article on why Jews join cults, and make a list of Jewish cults.

פִּינְחָס PINHAS

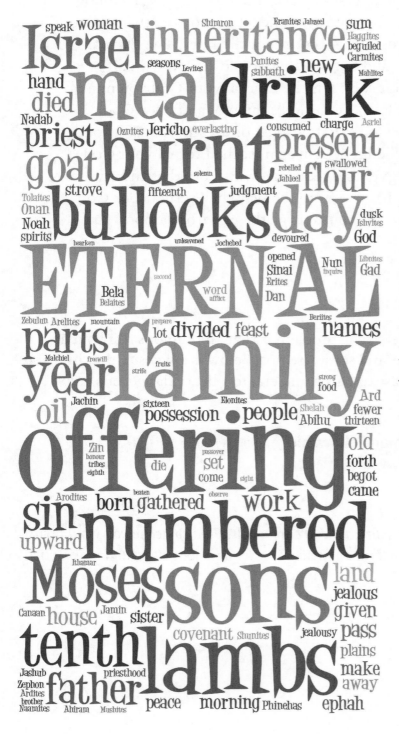

Overview: Numbers 25:10–30:1

Pinhas is rewarded for killing people who cursed God. Another census is taken in order to prepare for the war against the Midianites. The daughters of Zelophehad force a change in the laws of property inheritance to include daughters, not just sons, in inheritance. Joshua is chosen as Moses' successor. The *parashah* concludes with the listing of all the public sacrifices offered on the holy days.

OUR TORAH TEXT: NUMBERS 29:1

In this *sidrah* we get a cluster of holiday celebration practices. Among them is this favorite High Holy Day mitzvah:

וּבַחֹדֶשׁ הַשְּׁבִיעִי בְּאֶחָד לַחֹדֶשׁ מִקְרָא־קֹדֶשׁ
יִהְיֶה לָכֶם כָּל־מְלֶאכֶת עֲבֹדָה לֹא תַעֲשׂוּ
יוֹם תְּרוּעָה יִהְיֶה לָכֶם.

וּבחדש השביעי באחד לחדש מקרא
קדש יהיה לכם כל מלאכת עבודה
לא תעשו יום תרועה יהיה לכם

The first day of the seventh month will be to you a holy gathering. You will not do any work, and it will be a day of blowing the shofar.

Exploring Our Torah Text

The sound of the shofar is like a bugle call awakening us from our sleep. We are so busy with day-to-day interests, school, work, play, that we tend to become unaware of our true purpose in life, as though in a deep sleep. At Rosh ha-Shanah, when we start a new year, we are awakened to plan to do mitzvot and learn Torah during the coming year. Saadia Gaon pointed out ten different ways the shofar inspires us to live a better life in the new year.

1. When a new king begins to rule, a proclamation is issued, accompanied by trumpet blasts. Every year on that day his rule is again proclaimed, also with the sound of a trumpet. The creation of the world was completed on Rosh ha-Shanah, and God's rule of the world began.

Every year on that day we re-proclaim God's rule with the shofar's blast.

2. When a king issues a decree, the horns blow and a warning is announced. The Ten Days of T'shuvah (penitence) begin on Rosh ha-Shanah. "Improve your ways!" we are warned, and as this warning is issued, the shofar blows.

3. When Moses and the Children of Israel received the Torah on the slopes of Mt. Sinai, the sound of the shofar filled the air. On this day of Rosh ha-Shanah we dedicate ourselves to Torah again as the sound of the shofar fills the air.

4. The words of our prophets of old rang out like a shofar blast. We remind ourselves of their corrective words of ethical instruction when we hear the shofar blast.

5. Our enemies blew their trumpets when they destroyed our Holy Temple. When we blow the shofar on Rosh ha-Shanah we pray the new year will bring the rebuilding of the Temple to forgive us our sins.

6. Isaac willingly offered himself as a sacrifice, as God commanded, but at the last minute he was replaced by a ram. On Rosh ha-Shanah we blow on a ram's horn to remind ourselves and God of our ancestors' devotion.

7. "Could the shofar sound in the city, and the people not tremble with fright?" (Amos 3). The shofar makes us tremble in fear of God's judgment.

8. "Near is the great day of (judgment of) God; near, very quick, the day of the shofar" (Zefaniah 2). The Rosh ha-Shanah shofar reminds us of the final day of judgment.

9. "And it will be on that day the Great Shofar will be sounded, and the lost will come from the Land of Ashur, and the rejected from Egypt land" (Isaiah 23). The sound of the shofar reminds us of the Messiah's great horn. We hope and pray it be sounded this year to gather all the Jews scattered about the globe.

10. "The inhabitants of the dust...when the shofar will be heard" (Isaiah 18). The shofar reminds us of the day of when the dead will arise from their sleep.

Which of these metaphors for the sounding of the shofar do you find most powerful? Why? Which do you find least satisfying? Why?

Write you own meaning for hearing the shofar.

torah experience I

Have a shofar workshop.

- Find and watch a YouTube video on how to make a shofar.
- Find and watch a YouTube video on how to blow a shofar.
- Have everyone in class try to blow the shofar.

torah experience II

In an original midrash Rabbi Marc Gellman calls the shofar "The Announcing Tool." If you needed to create a modern "Announcing Tool," what would it be?

Reflection Question: What do you feel inside when you hear the shofar?

MITZVAH OF THE WEEK: שׁוֹפָר SHOFAR

It is a mitzvah to listen to the sound of a shofar (ram's horn) on Rosh ha-Shanah, the first day of Tishri.

> Laws: The horn of a non-kosher animal, a cow's horn or the horn of a wild animal may not be used as a shofar. It is preferable to use a ram's horn, and it is necessary that the horn be bent and not straight. If one reverses the shofar and blows in it from the wrong end, regardless of how he reverses it, he cannot fulfill his obligation. The sounds of the shofar are the *teki'ah*, a single, long note; the *sh'varim*, three shorter notes; and the *teru'ah*, a staccato sound, at least nine very short consecutive sounds.

It is the custom to sound one hundred notes on the shofar. These consist of thirty at the "sitting sounds" right after the initial brakhah; another thirty during the silent *Mussaf Amidah*; another thirty during the <u>h</u>azzan's repetition of the *Mussaf Amidah*, following, and finally, ten sounds during the *Kaddish* of the *Mussaf Amidah*. Hence 30 + 30 + 30 + 10 = 100.

Shofar Experience

In a midrash we are told that Satan went to Sarah and told her that her old husband had taken her son and was prepared to kill him. Isaac cried out when he saw the knife. And at the same time Sarah cried three cries. Her wailing sounded like three *teki-yot* on the shofar. Then she died. When Abraham came home he cried for Sarah (*Pirke d'Rabbi Eliezer*).

Write and perform an opera about the time that Abraham almost killed Isaac. Base your opera on this midrash.

Reflection Question: What was the difference between the three cries in this story?

Shofar Resources

Here are assorted sites that use the term "shofar" as a metaphor.

The Shofar Coalition
http://chanabaltimore.org/page.aspx?id=224665

The Shofar International Foundation
http://www.shofarintl.org/

Bend the Arc
http://bendthearc.us/news/releases/shofar-call-domestic-workers-rights

Shofar Flashmob
http://www.shofarflashmob.com/

Find the cheapest kosher shofar you can buy. What does it cost?

מטות Mattot

sheep heart Canaan flocks subdued mouth houses clean alive swore vengeance proceeds trumpets booty wander upward saved armed tribes wholly purify plague son forward wash swears brought cattle captains execute took away given iniquity married daughter offering women heard bond bound battle thing atonement brood followed cities Caleb commanded ones destroy Sebam camp lead send woman war wood burnt husband gave great skin skilled slew dwelt beast officers delivered goats oath know gold gift service enemies wives jewels vessels remain faith priest land hold lips heads bear brass Isaac dwell clear folds evil generation soul Moses iron holy valley forth little rest tent captives taken silver revolt hair parts anger kill afflict fallen favor half kept children fierce apart leave lacks kings alarm wilderness sinful near goods statutes spoil risen Israel father youth set encampments Mishkan pass bracelets Levites Jacob break stand vows divided ready eastward inhabitants Jericho void peace congregation divorced Joshua persons saw portion people gathered held sword driven day servants prey men work clothes place years armlets tribute touched hundreds inheritance meeting host

Overview: Numbers 30:2—32:42

Moses speaks to the heads of the Israelite tribes about oaths—those made by themselves, women, wives and widows. Israel fights against the Midianites. This provides the opportunity to teach some new laws: rules for dividing the spoils of war and rules for purifying warriors. The tribes of Gad and Reuven ask to stay on the East Bank of the Jordan River. Their rights and responsibilities are clarified.

OUR TORAH TEXT: NUMBERS 31:17

Genocide is a big word. It means murdering a whole people and trying to drive them out of existence. In this *parashah* we seem to find that in some cases, genocide is a mitzvah. This rule happens after the story of Balaam and relates to the war with Midian.

וְעַתָּה הִרְגוּ כָל־זָכָר בַּטָּף וְכָל־אִשָּׁה יֹדַעַת אִישׁ מִשְׁכַּב זָכָר הֲרֹגוּ.

ועתה הרגו כל זכר בטף כל אשה ידעת איש משכב זכר הרגו

Now kill all male children, and kill every woman that has known a man by sleeping with him.

Exploring Our Torah Text

By God's command, what were the Israelites supposed to do to the Midianites? (You may need to open your Bible and read more of the text to figure this out.)

1. What is your moral evaluation of this command? Is it morally justified in your eyes?

   To understand the ethics of this commandment, it is helpful to look at another mitzvah, "You shall utterly destroy them" (Deuteronomy 7:2). Interpreting this commandment, *Sefer ha-Ḥinukh* says:

   > It is a mitzvah to wipe out the seven nations who resided in *Eretz Yisrael* before the Families-of-Israel settled there. It is a mitzvah not to let any of them live.

   > The seven nations were the Hittites, Girgashites, Amorites, Canaanites, Perrizzites, Hivites and Jebusites. Those people of the seven nations who

202

sincerely agreed to give up their idolatry were allowed to remain unharmed.

2. Avraham Cronbach z"l was a leading American Reform rabbi during World War II. He was a founder of the Jewish Peace Fellowship. When asked about this commandment, he said, "I think this is a place where Moses misunderstood what God really wanted."

3. What is your own final take on this command to exterminate a non–Jewish people?

torah experience

There are lots of complaints about things that the Israeli army does. Most of that is government policy and not army behavior. Both the IDF (Israeli Defense Forces) and the Israeli courts hold the army to high ethical standards. Israel's army, the IDF, holds the following code of ethics:

The IDF Spirit

The Israel Defense Forces are the State of Israel's military force. The IDF is subordinate to the directions of the democratic civilian authorities and the laws of the state. The goal of the IDF is to protect the existence of the State of Israel and her independence, and to thwart all enemy efforts to disrupt the normal way of life in Israel. IDF soldiers are obligated to fight, to dedicate all their strength and even sacrifice their lives in order to protect the State of Israel, her citizens and residents. **IDF soldiers will operate according to the IDF values and orders, while adhering to the laws of the state and norms of human dignity, and honoring the values of the State of Israel as a Jewish and democratic state.**

Basic Values

Defense of the State, its Citizens and its Residents—The IDF's goal is to defend the existence of the State of Israel, its independence and the security of the citizens and residents of the state.

Love of the Homeland and Loyalty to the Country—At the core of service in the IDF stands the love of the homeland and the commitment and devotion to the State of Israel—a democratic state that serves as a national home for the Jewish people—its citizens and residents.

Human Dignity—The IDF and its soldiers are obligated to protect human dignity. Every human being is of value regardless of his or her origin, religion, nationality, gender, status or position.

Evaluate the commitments made by the Israeli army.

Reflection Question: What is your relationship with the Israeli army?

Genocide Resources

While we can find examples of genocide both against us and by us in the past, today most Jewish organizations are clearly anti-genocide. Elie Wiesel has made it clear that our experience with being victims during the Holocaust demands that we stand up and cry out against all human cruelty, especially genocide. Here are some anti-genocide websites.

Jewish World Watch
http://www.jewishworldwatch.org/

Stand
http://www.standnow.org/

World Without Genocide
http://worldwithoutgenocide.org/

List five genocides that are going on today.

MITZVAH OF THE WEEK: מִלְחֶמֶת מִצְוָה ETHICS IN WARFARE

In the Torah we are given a series of rules for war. We learn that some wars are commanded, some permitted and some forbidden. And we also learn that all wars have rules.

1. At first the king may wage only a mitzvah-war. Which wars are considered wars for mitzvah purposes? The war against the seven nations (of Canaan), the battle against Amalek and a defense of Israel from attacking enemies. Thereafter the king may wage an optional war, a war against other peoples, to extend Jewish territory and to augment his military prestige.

2. In the case of a mitzvah-war, the king does not have to obtain the sanction of the Supreme Court. He may at any time set out independently and compel the people to come out with him. But in the case of an optional war, he can bring out the people only by a decision of the court of seventy-one judges.

3. The king may break through anyone's property to make a road for himself, and no one may protest against him. No limit is prescribed for the king's road. He makes use of as much as he needs. He is not required to proceed by a detour because of somebody's vineyard or field. He takes the straight line and pursues his battles.

   No war is to be waged with anyone in the world before offering him terms of peace, whether it is an optional or a mitzvah-war, as it is written: "When you approach a town to attack it, you shall first offer it terms of peace" (Deuteronomy 20:10). If the inhabitants have responded peaceably and accepted the seven precepts imposed upon the descendants of Noah, none of them should be slain, but only taxed, as it is written: "They shall do forced labor for you and serve you." The tax imposed upon them consists in being prepared to serve the king physically and financially, as in the case of building walls and fortifying strongholds, or constructing a palace for the king, and the like.

4. It is forbidden to be false to the peace made with them, to deceive them when they have accepted the terms of peace and the seven precepts.

5. When a city is besieged in order to capture it, it must not be surrounded on all four sides but only on three sides, so as to leave room for a refugee and anyone who wishes to escape.

What would wars be like if armies really fought by these kinds of rules?

Experiencing the Ethics of War

The Values of the IDF

Tenacity of Purpose in Performing Missions and Drive to Victory: The IDF servicemen and women will fight and conduct themselves with courage in the face of all dangers and obstacles; they will persevere in their missions resolutely and thoughtfully even to the point of endangering their lives.

Responsibility: The IDF servicemen and women will see themselves as active participants in the defense of the state, its citizens and residents. They will carry out their duties at all times with initiative, involvement and diligence with common sense and within the framework of their authority, while prepared to bear responsibility for their conduct.

Credibility: The IDF servicemen and women shall present things objectively, completely and precisely, in planning, performing and reporting. They will act in such a manner that their peers and commanders can rely upon them in performing their tasks.

Personal Example: The IDF servicemen and women will comport themselves as required of them, and will demand of themselves as they demand of others, out of recognition of their ability and responsibility within the military and without to serve as a deserving role model.

Human Life: The IDF servicemen and women will act in a judicious and safe manner in all they do, out of recognition of the supreme value of human life. During combat they will endanger themselves and their comrades only to the extent required to carry out their mission.

Purity of Arms: The IDF servicemen and women will use their weapons and force only for the purpose of their mission, only to the necessary extent and will maintain their humanity even during combat. IDF soldiers will not use their weapons and force to harm human beings who are not combatants or prisoners of war, and will do all in their power to avoid causing harm to their lives, bodies, dignity and property.

Professionalism: The IDF servicemen and women will acquire the professional knowledge and skills required to perform their tasks, and will implement them while striving continuously to perfect their personal and collective achievements.

Discipline: The IDF servicemen and women will strive to the best of their ability to fully and successfully complete all that is required of them according to orders and their spirit. IDF soldiers will be meticulous in giving only lawful orders, and shall refrain from obeying blatantly illegal orders.

Comradeship: The IDF servicemen and women will act out of fraternity and devotion to their comrades, and will always go to their assistance when they need their help or depend on them, despite any danger or difficulty, even to the point of risking their lives.

Sense of Mission: The IDF soldiers view their service in the IDF as a mission; they will be ready to give their all in order to defend the state, its citizens and residents. This is due to the fact that they are representatives of the IDF who act on the basis and in the framework of the authority given to them in accordance with IDF orders.

Compare the values of the IDF to the values that the United States Army holds.

U.S. Army Values

Loyalty: Bear true faith and allegiance to the U.S. Constitution, the Army, and other soldiers. Be loyal to the nation and its heritage.

Duty: Fulfill your obligations. Accept responsibility for your own actions and those entrusted to your care. Find opportunities to improve oneself for the good of the group.

Respect: Rely upon the golden rule. How we consider others reflects upon each of us, both personally and as a professional organization.

Selfless Service: Put the welfare of the nation, the Army, and your subordinates before your own. Selfless service leads to organizational teamwork and encompasses discipline, self-control and faith in the system.

Adversity Along the Way: Hard physical labor characterized every day, but the Corps of Discovery conquered every navigational hazard and overcame a variety of physical ills.

Honor: Live up to all the Army values.

Importance of Character: Lewis and Clark were very thorough in selecting only the best men for the mission. Those who would work together for the good of the group and pull their own weight.

Integrity: Do what is right, legally and morally. Be willing to do what is right even when no one is looking. It is our moral compass, an inner voice.

Personal Courage: Our ability to face fear, danger or adversity, both physical and moral courage. Into the Unknown. The men of the Corps of Discovery left not knowing what lay ahead or if they would ever return. Throughout the journals one phrase stands out—"We proceeded on." This clearly characterizes the spirit of the expedition.

Reflection Question: Are there really war ethics, or is this an oxymoron?

Military Ethics Resources

One of the big issues in military ethics is land mines. Here are some organizations that face that issue.

Adopt-a-Landmine
http://www.adoptalandmine.org/

International Campaign to Ban Land Mines
http://www.icbl.org/

Stop Land Mines
http://www.stoplandmines.org

Find other categories of issues on the ethics of war.

שסעי MAS'EI

Overview:
Numbers
33:1—36:13

This is the eve of entering the Promised Land! Israel's journey from Egypt to the Jordan is reviewed. We are taught laws concerning the settlement of Canaan, including the boundaries of the Land of Israel, the Priestly Cities, and the Cities of Refuge. The distinction between murder and manslaughter is taught. We also learn of the laws of inheritance for women who marry men of other tribes.

OUR TORAH TEXT: NUMBERS 35:12

Mas'ei is the last Torah portion in Numbers. It tells of the last few moments of Jewish life in the wilderness. Included in it are a few laws about murder cases and a concept called Cities of Refuge.

וְהָיוּ לָכֶם הֶעָרִים לְמִקְלָט מִגֹּאֵל וְלֹא יָמוּת הָרֹצֵחַ עַד־עָמְדוֹ לִפְנֵי הָעֵדָה לַמִּשְׁפָּט.

והיו לכם הערים למקלט מגאל ולא ימות הרצח עד עמדו לפני העדה למשפט

And you should have cities of refuge from the revenge-seeker so that the person (who caused the death) will not die until he has stood before a gathering of justice (court).

Exploring Our Torah Text

When a man killed someone unintentionally he could find security by fleeing to one of the six cities. The blood avenger, who as next of kin to the slain person had the traditional task of hunting down the killer, could not violate the sanctuary of these cities. A trial would be held in the locale where the slaying occurred, and if lack of malice aforethought was established, the manslayer would be sent back to the city of refuge to stay there securely until the death of the reigning High Priest (Num. 35:25).

The Torah—A Modern Commentary, Gunther Plaut

1. Explain the concept of a City of Refuge.
2. Explain the need for Cities of Refuge.
3. What kinds of Cities of Refuge do we both have and need in our society?

eXPerieNCiNG our torAH teXt

Work in groups of four or five. Have everyone share a story of a time that they ran to a teacher, a parent or another adult to protect them.

Reflection Question: Why don't rules alone protect us? Why do humans need cities of refuge?

MITZVAH OF THE WEEK: שְׁנֵי עֵדִים TWO WITNESSES

Compare these two laws from the Codes to the two verdicts below.

From the *Mishneh Torah*: *Sanhedrin* 16.6

> The Torah teaches us (Ex. 23:1 /Deut. 19:15) that a court shall not find a man guilty through his own admission of guilt. This is done only on the evidence of two witnesses.

From the *Mishneh Torah*: *Sanhedrin* 20.1

> The court cannot find someone guilty on just circumstantial evidence, but only on the conclusive testimony of witnesses. Even if the witness saw the assailant chasing the victim, gave him a warning, and then lost sight of him, or followed him into a ruin and found the victim in death agony, while the sword dripping with blood was in the hands of the slayer, the court does not condemn the accused to death, since the witnesses did not see him at the time of the slaying.

Experiencing Shnei Aidim

Act out these cases.

Case 1—From the Responsa of Rabbi Simon ben Zemah Duran

FACTS: A blind man went on a trip with a companion who was a known criminal. They shared sleeping quarters. At the end of the trip a collection of gems was missing from the hem of the blind man's robe.

DECISION: Rabbi Simon suggests that the court throw the accused in jail until he confesses or until the gems are found. He explains, "It is well known that a thief does not practice his craft before witnesses! If we needed to limit prosecution of theft to those cases with valid witnesses, justice would be impaired." He based his argument on a story told in the Talmud, Bava Metzia 24a. A valuable object was stolen from Mar Zutra. Later he saw a rabbinical student wash his hands and dry them on someone else's clothes.

He said, "This one has no respect for personal property; he is the thief." The student was bound and later confessed. Rabbi Simon concludes his responsum, "I have already imprisoned a Jew of this place whom a traveler accused being a thief. The stolen article was later found in his possession, and I was praised by the community...."

Case 2—From the Responsa of Rabbi Israel ben Petahiah Isserlein

FACTS: Two men are known to be enemies. One threatens the other. During the dancing of the *Hoshana* celebrations on Sukkot, the party who was threatened was pushed and his shoulder broken. Leaving the synagogue, his enemy bragged about the revenge he had taken.

DECISION: Rabbi Israel begins, "We cannot impose liability... on the basis of supposition and circumstance." He goes on to explain selections of talmudic laws that prevent this. Still he concludes, "I am both intellectually and morally certain that this sort of incident requires significant preventative measures...it does appear and matters do demonstrate that R. Gershom did intend to injure and harm R. Eliezer..." Rabbi Israel's verdict came in three parts. The guilty party was required to pay for the medical expenses of the victim, pay a fine to tzedakah and publicly make atonement (accept responsibility and ask forgiveness) before the whole community.

What seems wrong with these verdicts?

Both of these responsa came from rabbis who were among the leading scholars of their era, who were authors of major halakhic works. They knew and followed Jewish law. How can you explain these verdicts?

This text is the key to solving this riddle.

> If one person kills another and there is no clear evidence, or if no warning has been given him, or there is only one witness, or if one accidentally kills a person whom he hated, the king may, if the situation calls for it, put him to death in order to ensure the stability of the social order. (Mishneh Torah, Kings 3:10)

Based on this text, how do you explain the responsa decisions on pages 210–211?

Reflection Question: Compare this with what you know of the American legal system, specifically the idea that you are innocent until proven guilty, and the setup of witnesses, juries and judges.

Shenei Eidim Resources

Here are the websites of organizations that work hard to bring people justice.

International Human Rights Center
http://www.icnl.org/

Bet Tzedek
http://www.bettzedek.org/

The Innocence Project
http://www.innocenceproject.org/

American Civil Liberties Union (ACLU)
http://www.aclu.org/

Human Rights Watch
http://www.hrw.org/

Who works for justice in your community? Find an organization. What can you do to help them?

דברים DEVARIM

Overview: Deuteronomy 1:1–3:22

The first portion of the last book of the Torah sets up what will occur throughout the book—a review of all that has happened since the Israelites left Egypt. This *parashah* specifically discusses the review of the journey from Sinai to Kadesh, the appointment of assistants for Moses, the journey to Horeb and then to Kadesh-Barne'a, the people's refusal to enter the Land of Canaan and the allotment of conquered land.

OUR TORAH TEXT: DEUTERONOMY 1:1

Our *sidrah* begins with Moses getting ready to die. He begins to reteach the whole Torah to the Jewish people.

אֵלֶּה הַדְּבָרִים אֲשֶׁר דִּבֶּר מֹשֶׁה אֶל־כָּל־יִשְׂרָאֵל
בְּעֵבֶר הַיַּרְדֵּן...

אלה הדברים אשר דבר משה אל כל
ישראל בעבר הירדן

These are the things that Moses said to all of Israel from across the Jordan...

Exploring Our Torah Text

Moses Assembles the People Before His Death

When God informed Moses that he would die after battling Midian, Moses requested, "Please, God, permit me to review the entire Torah with the people before my passing! I wish to clarify any difficulties they may have and to acquaint them thoroughly with the details of the Torah laws."

The Almighty honored Moses' request. On 1 Shevat 2488, thirty-seven days before Moses' death, He told him, "Assemble the people to review the mitzvot with them, and to instruct them in those mitzvot they have not yet heard from you."

Moses himself had learned all the mitzvot from God either at Mt. Sinai or in the first year after that in the Tent of Meeting (*Deuteronomy Rabbah 1:6*).

What Jewish practice is suggested by this piece of midrash?

tORAH eXPerIeNCe

Jews have developed a thing called an ethical will. A regular will speaks of to whom you will leave things. An ethical will is something you leave for your family and friends that is a collection of your wisdom and understandings.

Check out this ethical will on *YouTube*.

John from North Olmsted shares his Legacy
http://www.youtube.com/watch?v=E2XEpmso4tY

Have everyone in the class make notes and then record their own ethical wills.

Reflection Question: Why is an ethical will a good idea?

MITZVAH OF THE WEEK: שׁוֹפְטִים SHOFTIM

There are two mitzvot in this *parashah*. Both of them have to do with qualifications for judges. A rabbi was not only a teacher but could be a judge. The Torah needs to be understood as a book of law. Judaism wants to use courts to help people act well and be good people. If courts were that important, those who served as judges were equally important.

In this *sidrah* we learn that the following are among the qualifications of a judge: (a) knowing the Law, (b) knowing Torah, (c) being modest, (d) fearing God, (e) being respected by others, (f) being a seeker of truth, (g) not taking bribes and (h) not being afraid of litigants.

Shoftim Experience

Divide your class in half. Have one half made up of groups of three. Have the other half made up of groups of two. The threes are going to be judges in a Bet Din (a Jewish court); the twos are going to be litigants in a case they make up. In a Bet Din there are no lawyers. The judges do all the questioning. Run as many trials as groups. Have the judges work out and share a verdict (after asking all the questions they want).

Reflection Question: What is hard about judging?

Mishpat Resources

As long as we are talking about judges (*shoftim*), here are some justice (*mishpat*) resources.

American Consitution Society for Law and Policy
http://www.acslaw.org/

Public Justice Foundation
http://www.publicjustice.net/

Child Rights International Network
http://www.crin.org

Pick a social justice issue and find the URL of an organization that works on this issue.

וָאֶתְחַנַּן VA-ETHANNAN

Overview: Deuteronomy 3:23–7:11

Our *parashah* begins with one of the most famous scenes in the Torah. Moses is standing on the top of a mountain called Pisgah on the eastern side of the Jordan and is told to look west, north, south and east to view the land that he is not to enter. Although Moses prays to be allowed to enter the Land of Israel, God refuses, and that privilege is left to Joshua. Moses assigns three Cities of Refuge. We review the Sinai experience and the Ten Commandments. We are taught the *Shema* and *V'Ahavta*.

217

OUR TORAH TEXT: DEUTERONOMY 6:4

This *parashah* contains the first paragraph of the *Shema*. It has a lot of mitzvot hidden in it.

שְׁמַע יִשְׂרָאֵל יי אֱלֹהֵינוּ יי אֶחָד.

שמע ישראל יי אלהינו יי אחד

Listen Israel! The Eternal is our God. The Eternal is one.

Exploring Our Torah Text

Open a copy of the first paragraph of the *Shema*. (A siddur or a Torah will have it.) See how many mitzvot you can find hidden in the words.

TORAH EXPERIENCE

Bring in a consultant (if necessary) and have every student put on tefillin.

How did it feel?

Reflection Question: What can tefillin add to prayer?

MITZVAH OF THE WEEK: אֱמוּנָה FAITH

According to Maimonides, the *Shema* teaches that it is a mitzvah for us to believe in God. Maimonides created a famous list of thirteen things we should believe. Here are the first few.

The first is to believe in the existence of the Creator, Who-is-to-be-blessed. This means that there exists a Being that is complete in all ways and Who is the cause of all else that exists. God is what sustains their existence and the existence of all that sustains them. It is inconceivable that God would not exist. God does not need the existence of anything else. All that exists apart from God, the angels, the universe and all that is within it, all these things are dependent on God for their existence.

> This is taught to us in the statement, "I am the Eternal your God..." (Deuteronomy 5:6).

The second is to believe in the unity of God Who-is-to-be-blessed. In other words, to believe that this being, which is the cause of all, is one. This does not mean one as in one of a pair nor one like a species (that includes many individuals) nor one as in one object that is made up of many elements nor as a single simple object which is infinitely divisible. Rather, God Who-is-to-be-blessed, blessed be God's Name, is a unity unlike any other possible unity.

> This second is referred to when [the Torah] says "Listen Israel. The Eternal is our God. The Eternal is one" (Deuteronomy 6:4).

The third is that God is not physical. This means to believe that the One whom we have mentioned is not a body, and God's powers are not physical. The concepts of physical bodies such as movement, rest, or existence in a particular place cannot be applied to God. Therefore the Rabbis of blessed memory stated that the concepts of combination and separation do not apply to God, and they said, "Above there is no sitting nor standing, no separation nor combination." In all places where the Torah speaks of God in physical terms, such as walking, standing, sitting, speaking and anything similar, it is always metaphorical, as our Rabbis of blessed memory said, "The Torah speaks in the language of people."

List the three big ideas that Maimonides talks about here.

Emunah Experience

Find a partner. Share your beliefs about God with your partner.

Now gather in groups of six to eight. In these groups your partner should share your beliefs about God with the group.

Reflection Question: Is belief in God important? Why? Why not?

Emunah Resources

Take "One God." Add the fact that "all people are created in God's image." That makes every person responsible for everyone else. Here are the sites for several foundations devoted to the idea of one.

One
http://www.one.org/

1 World Foundation
http://www.1worldfoundation.info/

The One Foundation
http://www.onedifference.org/the-one-foundation

One World One Ocean Foundation
http://www.oneworldoneoceanfoundation.org/

One World One Heart Foundation
http://www.oneworldoneheartfoundation.com/

Find the URL of five foundations that honor being created in God's image.

עקב EKEV

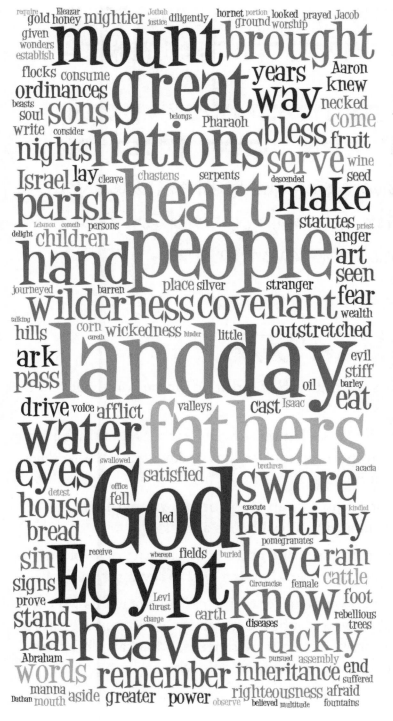

mount brought great way years Aaron knew necked come bless fruit wine seed serve nations make statutes anger art seen fear wealth heart people perish hand children wilderness covenant outstretched landday evil stiff barley eat oil water fathers eyes swore house God multiply bread sin love rain Egypt cattle signs know foot heaven quickly man remember inheritance end words righteousness afraid power

require gold honey Eleazar mightier Jotbah diligently hornet portion looked prayed Jacob ground worship given wonders establish flocks consume ordinances beasts soul write consider Pharaoh belongs nights Israel lay cleave chastens serpents descended Lebanon cometh persons delight place silver stranger journeyed barren talking hills corn wickedness hinder little ark pass drive voice afflict valleys cast Isaac swallowed brethren acacia detest office fell execute kindled led whereon fields buried pomegranates receive Circumcise female Levi thrust charge earth diseases rebellious trees prove stand Abraham pursued assembly suffered manna aside greater observe believed multitude fountains Dathan mouth

Overview: Deuteronomy 7:12–11:25

Ekev begins with the blessings that come from following God's laws and the consequences of not following the laws. Moses reminds the people not to be self-righteous and to learn the lessons of our history: following God's law brings us prosperity and health, and remembering our history should lead us to obedience to the laws and love of God.

221

OUR TORAH TEXT: DEUTERONOMY 8:10

This text talks about rules for what you have to do when you enter the land of Israel and start to live there. But hidden in these words is a daily mitzvah we know well.

וְאָכַלְתָּ וְשָׂבָעְתָּ וּבֵרַכְתָּ אֶת־יי אֱלֹהֶיךָ
עַל־הָאָרֶץ הַטֹּבָה אֲשֶׁר נָתַן־לָךְ.

וְאָכַלְתָּ וְשָׂבַעְתָּ וּבֵרַכְתָּ אֶת יי אֱלֹהֶיךָ
עַל הָאָרֶץ הַטֹּבָה אֲשֶׁר נָתַן לָךְ

When you have eaten and been satisfied you shall bless the Eternal your God for the good land which was given to you.

Exploring Our Torah Text

1. How does the mitzvah of *Birkat ha-Mazon* come out of our verse?

2. Maimonides was a famous Jewish teacher and thinker who wrote an important book on Jewish law called the *Mishneh Torah*. In it he says:

   > Anyone who eats any food or enjoys anything without saying a brakhah is a thief.

   If God created the world and lets us use part of it for our own needs, then a brakhah is a way of saying thank you.

3. The brakhah we say after eating can also teach us a second lesson. See if you can figure it out. If God lets us use part of what was created for our own needs, what can a brakhah after eating teach us about people who are hungry?

eXPeRIeNCING the toRAH

Birkat ha-Mazon is made up of four blessings. Work with a small group and decide what four things would you want to bless God for after eating.

Reflection Question: What are some of the top blessings you have in your life?

MITZVAH OF THE WEEK: בִּרְכַּת הַמָּזוֹן BIRKAT HA-MAZON

Birkat ha-Mazon is the flagship brakhah for the entire brakhah system. It is the one and only brakhah with a clean and precise biblical origin. All other brakhot evolve from *Birkat ha-Mazon*. The Torah says,

"After you have **eaten,** and you are **satisfied,** then you should **bless** the Eternal, your God" (Deuteronomy 8:10).

Reading rabbinically, the message is obvious. Step 1: Eat. Step 2: Be nourished. Step 3: Say *Birkat ha-Mazon*.

Rules of Birkat ha-Mazon

1. *Birkat ha-Mazon* must be said after every act of eating that involves a piece of bread that is the size of an olive or bigger.

2. When three or more adults have eaten together *Birkat ha-Mazon* should be said together. The *zimmun* is added when three or more eat and bless together *(Brakhot 7:1)*. When ten or more join in *zimmun*, the word *Eloheinu* is added to the text.

3. *Birkat ha-Mazon* must be said where a meal is eaten—part of making the table into an altar *(Brakhot 8:7)*.

4. The tablecloth should be left on the table during *Birkat ha-Mazon*. Knives should be removed or covered.

Experiencing Birkat ha-Mazon

As a class, create a *Birkat ha-Mazon* booklet.

1. Study some *Birkat ha-Mazon* booklets.
2. In committees, prepare the text.
3. Make drawings to decorate the pages.
4. Make sure that you copy enough copies.
5. Eat a meal together.
6. Say *Birkat ha-Mazon* from your booklet.

Birkat ha-Mazon Resources

Here are some stop hunger websites.

Trickle Up
http://www.trickleup.org

Freedom from Hunger
http://www.freedomfromhunger.org/

Stop Hunger Now
http://www.stophungernow.org

Find a Jewishly sponsored hunger organization. Report on Global Hunger Shabbat.

ראה RE'EH

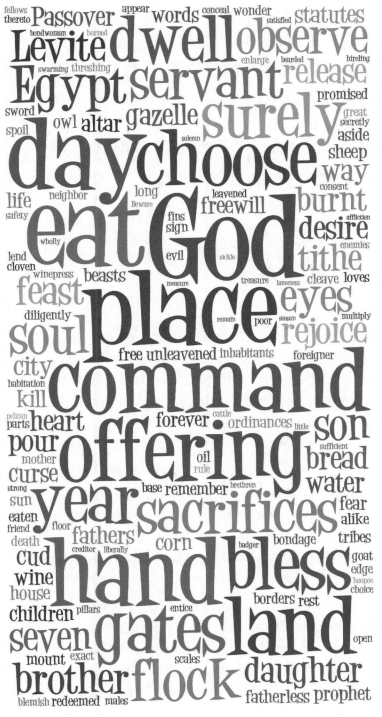

fellows Passover appear words conceal wonder statutes
thereto Levite bondwoman horned d well observe satisfied
Egypt swarming threshing servant enlarge bearded release hireling
sword gazelle surely great secretly promised
spoil owl altar solemn aside sheep
day choose way consent
life neighbor long leavened burnt
safety Beware freewill fins desire affliction
lend wholly evil sign God sickle tithe enemies
cloven winepress beasts measure treasure lameness cleave loves
feast place eyes
diligently soul free unleavened inhabitants remain poor season rejoice multiply
city foreigner
habitation command little
kill pelican parts heart forever cattle ordinances son
pour offering oil rule sufficient bread
mother curse base remember brethren water
strong year sacrifices fear
sun eaten floor alike
friend fathers corn badger bondage tribes
death cud creditor liberally goat
wine hand bless edge
house hoopoe choice
children pillars entice borders rest
seven gates land open
mount exact scales
brother flock daughter
blemish redeemed males fatherless prophet

Overview: Deuteronomy 11:26–16:17

God sets before us the classic choice, offering us blessing if we follow God's commandments and curses if we do not. God tells us to be a holy (*kadosh*) nation in our eating practices, in how we treat our bodies, in how we distribute wealth, in how we preserve our natural resources and in the role of the firstborn. The *parashah* ends with a review of the pilgrimage festivals (Passover, Shavuot and Sukkot), describing the mitzvah to journey to the central place of worship.

OUR TORAH TEXT: DEUTERONOMY 15:8

This verse is the place where everyones favorite mitzvah, giving tzedakah, is anchored in the Torah.

כִּי־פָתֹחַ תִּפְתַּח אֶת־יָדְךָ לוֹ וְהַעֲבֵט תַּעֲבִיטֶנּוּ
דֵּי מַחְסֹרוֹ אֲשֶׁר יֶחְסַר לוֹ .

כי פתח תפתח את ידך לו והעבט
תעביטנו די מחסרו אשר יחסר לו

Open your hand to that person and lend that person enough for his or her needs.

Exploring Our Torah Text
Jewish Sources

[1] If a poor stranger comes to you and says, "I am hungry, give me something to eat," you should not suspect the stranger. Rather feed him or her immediately. If, however, the stranger has no clothing and says, "Clothe me," the stranger's claim should be checked (*Mishneh Torah, Laws of Gifts to the Poor, 6.6*).

[2] Levi Yitzhak was the rabbi of the town of Berditchev. Once he was invited to a meeting to discuss the following new procedure: In order to keep the poor from begging door to door, a box was placed in the synagogue. Each person would then put in according to her or his abilities. And the poor would take out according to their needs.

Rabbi Levi Yitzhak was angry. He said, "There is nothing new in this procedure. It is very, very old. It started in the city of Sodom. There they had a community charity box where the well-to-do could leave their donations—and no one had to look his or her poor brothers or sisters in the eye" (*Tiferet Bet Levi*).

Use the internet and find two more quotations about tzedakah to add to this section.

226

torah experience

Using the case below, stage a courtroom in the classroom to adjudicate the case. You'll need a judge, lawyers for both sides and a jury. If you have a big class, you might consider having witnesses or experts present as well.

The Case: Young v. New York City Transit Authority, CA 2, No. 90-7115, 5/10/90; rev'g 58 LW 2456

The New York City Transit Authority issued a regulation that banned begging and panhandling in New York City subways. It did, however, allow organized charities to solicit funds. A beggar named Young challenged the legality of this regulation, and the case was heard before the New York State Supreme Court.

MITZVAH OF THE WEEK: צְדָקָה TZEDAKAH

Sometimes the origins of a word can teach us a lot. The English word that is closest to tzedakah is "justice," but when we talk about giving money to help those who are in need, the words "charity" and "philanthropy" are often used. See if you can find the difference in their meanings.

TZEDAKAH (Hebrew)

TZEDEK = justice, righteousness

CHARITY (Latin) caritas = love, fondness

PHILANTHROPY (Greek) philia = love + anthropos = people

KEREN AMI (Hebrew) My People's Fund

Based on their root meanings, what is the difference between the Jewish mitzvah of giving tzedakah and the practice of giving charity or philanthropy?

Tzedakah Experience

Rabbi Moses Maimonides was one of the greatest Jewish scholars of all times. He spent much of his time writing books that help Jews apply the laws and teaching of the Torah to the way they live and treat other people. This text from one of his books of law, the *Mishneh Torah*, is the way he solved the problem of the tzedakah contest.

There are eight different ways of giving tzedakah, and each way is better than the one that comes after it.

Take these eight rungs and put them in what you believe is the best order.

____ The next best case is the person who gives money directly to the person in need before the person has to ask.

____ The next best way of giving tzedakah is where the person who gives doesn't know who will receive the money, and the person who receives the money doesn't know who has given it.

____ The next best case is a person who gives directly to the poor person but gives less than he or she should, even though the tzedakah is given cheerfully.

____ The next best way of giving tzedakah is where the person who gives knows who will get the money, but the person who receives the tzedakah doesn't know who gave it.

____ The best way of giving is to help a person help him/herself by entering into a partnership or helping that person find a job.

____ The next best case is the person who gives tzedakah with a scowl. No matter how it is given, giving tzedakah is a mitzvah.

____ The next best case is the person who gives money directly to the person in need after being asked.

____ The next best case is one where the person who receives the tzedakah knows who has given it, but the person who is giving the tzedakah has no knowledge of the person in need.

Reflection Question: What is the best way to teach a person how to fish?

Tzedakah Resources

In the United States we talk about "not for profits" or 501c3s (a tax status). Elsewhere they speak about NGOs (non-governmental organizations). They are the same. They are groups that are designed to improve situations. Some of these are funded by families or corporations; most of them are looking for funds. Giving to them is a kind of tzedakah. Here are a few of my favorites that haven't yet fit into this book.

One Laptop per Child
http://one.laptop.org/

Wounded Warrior Project
http://www.woundedwarriorproject.org/

techsoup
http://www.techsoup.org/

Repair the World
http://werepair.org/

Find some good criteria for making decisions about the organizations to which a person gives.

שופטים SHOFTIM

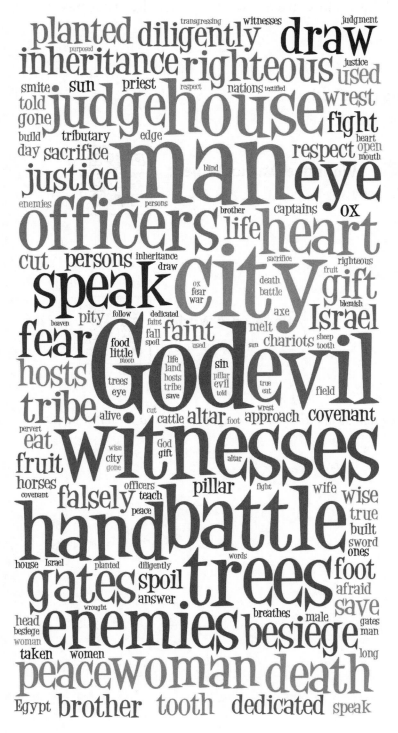

planted diligently transgressing witnesses draw judgment
inheritance purposed righteous justice used
smite sun priest respect nations testified wrest
told judge house fight
gone build tributary edge heart open mouth
day sacrifice man eye
justice blind respect
enemies officers persons brother captains ox
cut persons inheritance life heart
speak draw city sacrifice righteous
pity follow dedicated death fruit gift blemish
heaven faint battle melt Israel
fear food little fall spoil used sun chariots sheep tooth
hosts trees God evil true field
tribe eye land hosts tribe save pillar evil told wrest
alive cut cattle altar foot approach covenant
pervert wise city God witnesses gift altar
eat fruit gone
horses officers pillar fight wife wise
covenant falsely teach peace true
hand battle built sword
house Israel planted diligently words ones
gates trees foot afraid
wrought spoil answer save
head besiege enemies breathes male besiege man gates
taken women woman long
peace woman death
Egypt brother tooth dedicated speak

Overview: Deuteronomy 16:18–21:9

More laws are reviewed: the appointment of judges, laws against worshipping idols, laws concerning the high court, king, priests and Levites, criminal laws and the laws of warfare.

230

OUR TORAH TEXT: DEUTERONOMY 20:19

In this *sidrah* we get some Jewish rules of war. In our verse a war rule has big ecological ramifications.

כִּי־תָצוּר אֶל־עִיר יָמִים רַבִּים לְהִלָּחֵם עָלֶיהָ
לְתָפְשָׂהּ לֹא־תַשְׁחִית אֶת־עֵצָהּ לִנְדֹּחַ עָלָיו גַּרְזֶן
כִּי מִמֶּנּוּ תֹאכֵל וְאֹתוֹ לֹא תִכְרֹת כִּי הָאָדָם עֵץ
הַשָּׂדֶה לָבֹא מִפָּנֶיךָ בַּמָּצוֹר.

כי תצור אל עיר ימים רבים להלחם
עליה לתפשה לא תשחית את עצה
לנדח עליו גרזן כי ממנו תאכל ואתו
ולא תכרת כי האדם עץ השדה לבא
מפניך במצור

When you besiege a city for a long time, making war against it in order to capture it, you shall not destroy (*lo tash'hit*) the trees by wielding an axe against them, for you may eat of them. You should not cut them down. Are the trees in the field people that they should be attacked by you?

Exploring Our Torah Text

This verse travels through Jewish history and grows into a completely different set of practices. Look at how it expands.

Here are five Jewish sources for our verse and those that have grown out of it.

Number them in the order in which you think they were written.

_____ **Text A. *Kiddushin* 32a:** Whoever breaks vessels, or tears garments, or destroys a building, or clogs up a well, or does away with food in a destructive manner violates the negative mitzvah of *bal tash-hit* (do not waste).

_____ **Text B. *Mishneh Torah*, Mourning 14:24:** One should be trained not to be destructive. When you bury a person do not waste garments by burying them in the grave. It is better to give them to the poor than to cast them to worms and moths. Anyone who buries the dead in an expensive garment violates the negative mitzvah of *bal tash'hit*.

_____ **Text C. *Shevi'ith* 4:10:** How much fruit should an olive tree produce so that it may be considered a fruit-bearing tree and should not be cut down *(lo tash'hit)*? Rabbi Simeon ben Gamaliel taught a *rova* (1 *rova* = 33.6 cubic inches).

_____ **Text D. Deuteronomy 20:19–20:** When you besiege a city for a long time, making war against it in order to capture it, you shall not destroy *(lo tash'hit)* the trees by wielding an axe against them, for you may eat of them. You should not cut them down. Are the trees in the field people that they should be besieged by you?

_____ **Text E. *Shulhan Arukh*, Laws of Body and Soul, Section 14:** It is forbidden to destroy anything that can be useful to people.

Create a text timeline using the texts above.

a. Ask [the students] to read the texts and try to guess the order in which they were written.

b. Next read page 233 together.

c. Have the students create a timeline of the texts, reprinting each quote and hanging them along the wall.

d. Then have the students illustrate their understanding of the text on each poster.

Background History Of Sources

The Bible. All of Jewish law is based on the Bible. The Bible is made up of three parts: the Torah, the Prophets and the Writings. The Torah especially is filled with laws and rules about the ways people should live together. The Bible, however, was written for a period when most Jews were farmers. It was a time when life was simple, when there was little business and almost no cities.

The *Mishnah* is the first part of the Talmud. It was written by a group of scholars called the Rabbis who lived between 200 B.C.E. and 200 C.E. The *Mishnah* is divided into six orders, and there are many books in each of these orders. The *Mishnah* groups laws found in the Bible and adds and adapts laws for later societies. In the *Mishnah*, almost every word is part of a simple statement of the rule and its application.

The *Gemara* is the second part of the Talmud. Between 200 and 500 C.E. additional Rabbis added their own comments to the *Mishnah*. This updating and expansion of the *Mishnah* again helped to adapt the laws to the latest changes and problems in society. Unlike the *Mishnah*, which is basically a direct law code, the *Gemara* is filled with dialogue, stories and other interesting tangents. The Talmud (*Mishnah* and *Gemara* together) forms the heart of the Jewish legal process.

The Codes. As the times changed people had questions about how the laws of the Talmud should be applied in their day and in their situation. They ran into two problems. First, as society continued to change and evolve, new problems arose that called for new interpretations. Second, it was often difficult to find a particular law in the Talmud. The solution came with the creation of the Codes. The Codes were books that organized the law by subject and included all the rules that had been added to deal with new situations. While there are many Codes of Jewish law, the two most famous are the *Mishneh Torah*, which was written by Maimonides (Moses ben Maimon) in the twelfth century, and the *Shulḥan Arukh*, which was written in the sixteenth century by Joseph Caro.

The Responsa. Meanwhile, the Jewish legal process didn't stop with the Codes. People still faced situations that demanded interpretations of the law. When a local rabbi felt unable to work out a correct answer he would draft a letter to a leading scholar. These letters and their answers were collected as volumes of Responsa. These, too, became part of the literature Jews consult to find the right application of the Torah to their situation.

THE MITZVAH OF THE WEEK: בַּל תַּשְׁחִית BAL TASH'HIT

Write your own description of this mitzvah.

Experiencing Bal Tash'hit—a Sh'elah

The following letter was sent by the board of a synagogue to a famous scholar—one of the leading rabbis of this generation. The congregation whose board composed the letter was faced with a Jewish legal question they didn't know how to answer. To find a solution they followed an ancient Jewish practice of consulting an outstanding *halakhic* figure of their generation.

There is a whole body of Jewish literature made up of letters requesting legal advice and answers received. These are called responsa. Each responsum is made up of two parts: the *sh'elah* (the request) and the *t'shuvah* (the answer).

Dear Rabbi:

We seek your counsel in helping this congregation resolve a question of great moral and practical significance.

Like many congregations, our synagogue has a contract with a caterer who has the exclusive right to provide food for functions in our social hall. For this privilege Mr. Reuben pays an annual fee and donates a fixed percentage of his income to the congregation. He is also expected to provide certain free food services to the congregation. He is a good man, and the relationship is indeed beneficial to the community.

In our community there is a shelter that houses and feeds those without homes. Our congregation makes regular donations to this shelter, and some of the members volunteer time there. Recently the shelter requested that we turn over food that is left over after weddings and b'nai mitzvah celebrations. Normally this food is thrown out, since state health codes forbid it being served again.

Based on this request, our board enacted a congregational policy that all leftover foods would indeed be donated to the shelter. When this policy was presented to our caterer, he refused to follow it. He explained that it would cost him substantial time and money to make this food available. Most of our board is also in business and, understanding the caterer's position, reversed the policy.

When our rabbi learned of the change, he instructed the board that there is a principle of Jewish law called *bal tash'hit* that forbids Jews to waste any valuable resource. He said that it was our obligation to see to it that this food was not destroyed. While his position seems correct morally, it seems unfair to ask either

234

the congregation or the caterer to bear the expense of making this food available. Our rabbi suggested that we write to you and seek your insight. Thank you.

The board of Anshei Ḥesed

When a rabbi writes a *t'shuvah* (response) to a legal problem, he or she doesn't just give her/his own opinions. Writing a halakhic response is a research project. A rabbi checks all previous sources and finds the cases and laws that apply.

Write your own *t'shuvah* (response) to this letter.

Bal Tash'hit Resources

Here are a few of many foundations that work on not wasting the environment.

Audubon Society
http://www.audubon.org/

Foundation for Deep Ecology
http://www.deepecology.org/

Sea Save
http://seasave.org/

Wood's Hole Oceanographic Institute
http://www.whoi.edu/

Find two more organizations that work on the environment.

כי תצא KI TETZE

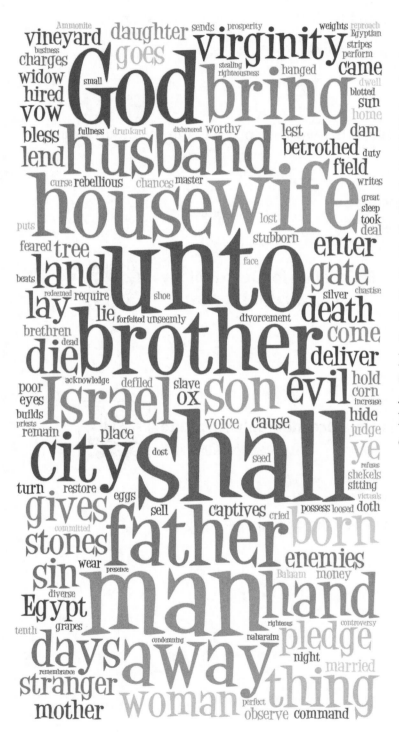

Another *parashah* where laws are reviewed: family laws (including marriage, rights of the firstborn and the disobedient child), laws of kindness, laws of returning lost property. From here until the end of the *parashah* there is a miscellaneous collection of laws, among which are sparing the mother bird, parapets on rooftops, unlike animals working together, *shaatnez* (mixing of certain kinds of materials in clothing) and *tzitzit*.

OUR TORAH TEXT: DEUTERONOMY 22:1

This *parashah* is once again Moses reviewing basic Jewish laws. All Jewish laws of lost and found come from this verse.

לֹא־תִרְאֶה אֶת־שׁוֹר אָחִיךָ אוֹ אֶת־שֵׂיוֹ נִדָּחִים וְהִתְעַלַּמְתָּ מֵהֶם הָשֵׁב תְּשִׁיבֵם לְאָחִיךָ.

לא תראה את שׁוֹר אזיך או את שׂיו נדזים והתעלמת מהם השב תשיבם לאזיך

You shall not see you neighbor's ox or sheep wandering and hide yourself from the responsibility for them. You must bring them back to your neighbor.

EXPERIENCING THE TORAH

Form small groups. Make a list of rules for lost and found. What can be kept? What should you try to return? What should be put in a central collection? How do you try to find the owner?

After your small groups have met, have a class meeting. Make a set of class rules about lost and found.

Exploring Our Torah Text

These two pieces of Mishnah expand our verse by stating when a finder must try to return a lost object and when the lost object may be kept.

Bava Metzia 2.1

If a person finds a lost object, when may the finder keep the object, and when must the found object be publicly advertised?

The following objects belong to the finder:

> scattered fruit
> scattered money
> small sheaves of grain (on a public street)
> cakes of figs
> loaves of bakers' bread
> strings of fish
> pieces of meat
> bundles of combed flax
> strips of purple wool

These belong to the finder, according to Rabbi Meir.

Rabbi Judah says, "Everything that has personal markings or changes must be publicly advertised."

"Explain!"

"For example, if one finds a bundle of figs with a potsherd in it or a loaf with a coin in it." Rabbi Shimon ben Elazar says, "All brand-new items with no identification or sign of use need not be advertised."

Bava Metzia 2.2

The following must be advertised as found by the finder.

fruit in a container or just an empty container

> money in a bag or just an empty bag
> a pile of fruit
> a pile of money
> three coins on top of each other
> small sheaves of grain in a private area
> homemade loaves of bread

238

These must be advertised.

Restate the basic principles in your own words.

A finder may keep a lost object when _____

_____

A finder must try to return a lost object when _____

_____

Make posters that remind students to bring found objects to the school office. Posters should include some Jewish text explanation of why it is important to return found items.

Reflection Question: Why are laws about lost and found important?

MITZVAH OF THE WEEK: RETURNING LOST OBJECTS

It is a mitzvah to return lost property to its owner. One is obligated to return a fellow Jew's lost property even if it is worth as little as a shekel (the value of a piece of silver weighing the same as half a grain of barley). The finder is obligated to care for the found article until it is claimed by its rightful owner. If it is something that may deteriorate or die, such as fresh food or an ill animal, he may sell it and hold the money for the owner. In the interim the finder is required to make the public aware of his finding. In earlier times these announcements were made after davening or between *Minhah* and *Ma'ariv*. Nowadays notices are posted on the bulletin board in the local shul.

The owner may claim the lost article only if he can properly identify it by a unique characteristic or a definitive description of the object, such as size, color or some kind of imperfection. This mitzvah applies even to real property. For example, if one sees that an onrushing river is about to demolish the home or field of a fellow Jew, he must work intensely to put up a dam in order to prevent a disaster.

Experiencing Lost and Found

Use your understanding of these two *mishnayot* to explain what should be done with each of these found objects. Put a **K** in front of every item you can keep. Put an **A** in front of every item you must advertise. Circle every case in which you think the Mishnah's categories should be reconsidered.

_____ A) A wallet with $5 and no identification found on the floor of a classroom with eighteen students and one teacher.

_____ B) A wallet with $5 and no identification found on the floor of a cafeteria of a company with 250 employees.

_____ C) A wallet with $5 and no identification found in Madison Square Garden.

_____ D) A bag of groceries left on a bus stop bench.

_____ E) Two bleachers tickets to a World Series baseball game.

_____ F) A six-pack of diet cola left on a mailbox.

_____ G) A briefcase left in a taxi.

_____ H) A briefcase left in a synagogue boardroom.

_____ I) A bag with six of the latest CDs, all unopened.

_____ J) A homemade green sweater with the name Buzz woven into the sleeve.

_____ K) A green polo sweater (size medium).

_____ L) A lottery ticket.

_____ M) Tickets 137 through 145 to the Beth El Congregation dinner with the name Heller written on the back of the first ticket.

_____ N) A blank DVD left in a DVD player you rented.

_____ O) Three sheets of brand-new plywood sitting in a vacant lot.

_____ P) An empty gym bag left in the lobby of an apartment building.

_____ Q) An empty gym bag left by a basketball court in a public park.

_____ R) $25 in quarters spilled in the alley.

_____ S) A briefcase with $5,000 left behind under a park bench.

_____ T) A bundle of figs and a potsherd left in the middle of a shopping center.

_____ U) A pair of expensive skis (which probably fell off a car roof) sitting by the side of the road. On each is the mark H.I. Stu.

_____ V) A brand new iPod, still in the box, left on the railing of a freeway overpass.

_____ W) A case of baseball bats left in an alley.

240

_____ X) A dog found at the back door without any identification tags.

_____ Y) A rough draft of an essay for a competition with the initials D.M.

_____ Z) A golf ball with "Love, Joanne" imprinted in gold letters, found near a public golf course.

Rabbi Morley Feinstein, *The Jewish Law Review*

Lost And Found Resources

Finding and redeeming is a kind of lost and found. Here are a few of many rescue foundations.

Rescue Foundation
http://www.rescuefoundation.net/

Lost Dog and Cat Rescue Foundation
http://www.lostdogandcatrescue.org/

Search Dog Foundation
http://www.searchdogfoundation.org/

Most animal rescue organizations are local. Find one in your area. Pick out a pet you might want to adopt.

כִּי תָבוֹא KI TAVO

This portion acknowledges God as the giver of all, to whom we pay tribute with first fruits and other sacrifices. The laws of first fruits and tithes are reviewed, descriptions of three tithes (to the Levites, to the owner of Jerusalem and to the poor and dependent) are given. We are instructed on how to cross the Jordan River, and that we must build an altar immediately after crossing.

242

OUR TORAH TEXT: DEUTERONOMY 28:9

Having retaught most of the laws, Moses launches into his big sermon.

יְקִימְךָ יי לוֹ לְעַם קָדוֹשׁ כַּאֲשֶׁר נִשְׁבַּע-לָךְ
כִּי תִשְׁמֹר אֶת-מִצְוֹת יי אֱלֹהֶיךָ וְהָלַכְתָּ בִּדְרָכָיו.

יְקִימְךָ יי לוֹ לְעַם קָדוֹשׁ כַּאֲשֶׁר נִשְׁבַּע
לָךְ כִּי תִשְׁמֹר אֶת מִצְוֹת יי אֱלֹהֶיךָ
וְהָלַכְתָּ בִּדְרָכָיו

The Eternal will make you into a holy people to God, as God has promised to do, if you will keep the mitzvot of the Eternal your God and walk in God's ways.

torah experience

People are created in God's image. God has no physicality. People are created with the ability to behave like God and be good. Make a list of values that describe God.

Reflection Question: If God can't walk, what does it mean to walk in God's ways?

243

Exploring Our Torah Text

The real meaning is to walk after the attributes of the Holy One.

> As God clothes the naked, so should you also clothe the naked, for it is written, "The Eternal, the God, made for Adam and for his wife coats of skin, and clothed them."
>
> The Holy One visited the sick, so should you also visit the sick, for it is written, "The Eternal appeared to Abraham after his circumcision by the oaks of Mamre."
>
> The Holy One comforted mourners, so should you also comfort mourners, for it is written, "And it came to pass after the death of Abraham that God blessed Isaac his son."
>
> The Holy One buried the dead, so should you also bury the dead, for it is written, "And God buried Moses in the valley."

Based on this interpretation in the Talmud, what mitzvah is found here?

MITZVAH OF THE WEEK: וְהָלַכְתָּ בִּדְרָכָיו WALKING AFTER GOD

It is a mitzvah to emulate God's righteous ways. One should strive to perfect oneself in the following character traits: compassion, kindness and graciousness towards others; forgiveness for iniquity; honesty, humility and tolerance (*Sefer ha-Hinukh*).

Experiencing V'halakhta B'drakhav

Look up these two passages in the Torah.

Genesis 1:27 _____

Exodus 34:6 _____

How do they expand our understanding of this mitzvah?

List ten things you can do to fulfill this mitzvah.

V'halakhta B'drakhav Resources

Walks, rides and runs are ways of raising money, particularly to cure diseases. Here are some URLs of foundations about walking.

Avon Walk for Breast Cancer
http://www.avonwalk.org/

Everybody Walk
http://www.everybodywalk.org/

Wheel to Walk Foundation
http://www.wheeltowalk.com/

Walk Strong Foundation
http://www.walkstrongfoundation.org/

נצבים NITZAVIM

scattered wood children woman means blessing ● ETERNAL allotted swept
midst heaven nations idols grows
serve ones sicknesses
persecuted compassion mouth bring
indignation revealed drawn burning pass
away curse heat surely
oath Sodom dispersed gall seed
love circumcise cast soul blot grass forever set
walk gold dry nigh hate voice curse fetch
live heart pass land cleave
Israel drawer earth jealousy hard
family turn come
lest shall land
little book God covenant rooted pardon fruit
written salt swore
command swore life
seen enter stubbornness declare went
fathers lie away anger sea
rise generation nations silver unto kindled parts
turn day bring hear
body separate evil goes shall secret cattle witness
driven foreigner return ways
bears ordinances come
great anger
elders Jordan dwell make officers sown good
tribes covenant fathers establish
willing heaven choose brimstone
wrath blessing far make
death peace perish
hand voice things possess
work overthrow command plagues hearken saying
written knew law things prolong hearken
law length hearken

Overview: Deuteronomy 29:9–30:20

Moses speaks to all Israelites who have entered and will enter into the covenant. He explains that God does not want to punish the Families-of-Israel; if we seek God, God will show mercy. Moses explains that God's commandments are not hard and distant, but practical to follow, and very close to us.

OUR TORAH TEXT: DEUTERONOMY 30:19

Moses' life is almost over. He is finishing up his State of the Wilderness speech. Our verse is one of the great sound bites from that address.

הַעִידֹתִי בָכֶם הַיּוֹם אֶת־הַשָּׁמַיִם וְאֶת־הָאָרֶץ
הַחַיִּים הַמָּוֶת נָתַתִּי לְפָנֶיךָ הַבְּרָכָה וְהַקְּלָלָה
וּבָחַרְתָּ בַּחַיִּים לְמַעַן תִּחְיֶה אַתָּה וְזַרְעֶךָ.

הַעִידֹתִי בכם היום את השמים ואת
הארץ הַחיים הַמות נתתי לפניך
הברכה והקללה ובחרת בחיים לְמעַן
תחיה אתה וזרעך

I call Heaven and Earth to witness against you, that I have given you a choice, that I have placed before you—life, the blessing, and death, the curse—choose life that you will live, you and your descendants after you.

247

Exploring our Torah Text

Whether or Not to Fight on Shabbat (1 Maccabees, chapter 2, verses 31–41)

This story took place during the beginning of the Jews' rebellion against the Greeks (during the Hanukkah story). The Maccabees were just being formed. Before they were organized, some Jews had already begun to fight back.

> Word soon reached the king's officers and the forces in Jerusalem, the city of David, that Jews who had defied the king's order had gone down into hiding places in the wilds. A large group of soldiers went quickly after and found them and occupied a position opposite. The soldiers prepared to attack them on the Sabbath.
>
> "There is still time," the soldiers shouted. "Come out, obey the king's command and your lives will be spared."
>
> "We will not come out," the Jews replied. "We will not obey the king's command or profane the Sabbath."

These Jews had fought back against the Greeks in order to follow Jewish law and observe Jewish customs. They had a hard choice to make. In order to win their fight for religious freedom, they would have to break the very Jewish laws they were fighting to defend.

If you were one of these Jewish rebels in the forest, would you break Shabbat and fight back against the Greeks? Why?

torah experience

This is what actually happened (at least this is the way the story is told in the first book of Maccabees).

> Without more ado the attack was launched; but the Jews did nothing in reply; they neither hurled stones nor barricaded their caves. "Let us meet death with a clear conscience," they said.

So they were attacked and massacred on the Sabbath, men, women and children, up to a thousand in all, and their cattle with them.

Great was the grief of Mattathias and his friends when they heard the news. They said to one another, "If we all do as our brothers have done, if we refuse to fight the king's soldiers for our lives as well as for our laws and customs, then they will soon wipe us off the face of the earth."

That day they decided that if anyone came to fight against them on the Sabbath, they would fight back rather than all die as their brothers in the caves had done.

Have a debate. Resolved: The Jews did the right thing by not fighting back on Shabbat.

Reflection Question: What is the relationship between saving a life and other Jewish rules?

MITZVAH OF THE WEEK: פְּקוּחַ נֶפֶשׁ PIKU'AH NEFESH

The obligation to save another person is based on a principle in *halakhah* (Jewish law) called *Pikuah Nefesh,* saving a soul. Protecting a human life is a major Jewish obligation.

Our rabbis learned this lesson from the Torah:

> Do not stand idly by the blood of your neighbor (Leviticus 19:16).

Leviticus 19:16 teaches us that as Jews we are not allowed to stand by and watch someone else be injured or killed. That would be "standing idly by the blood of your neighbor." If someone is going to be hurt or killed, a Jew must try to prevent this injury or death. This is the same idea as choosing life.

The Mishnah says: "Whenever a human life is endangered, the laws of the Sabbath are suspended."

The more eagerly someone goes about saving a life, the more worthy he or she is of praise.

If a person sees a child fall into the sea on the Sabbath, he or she may spread a net and rescue the child—the sooner the better—and he or she need not get permission from a court of law, even though in spreading the net he or she may also catch fish (which is forbidden on the Sabbath).

If a person sees a child fall into a pit, he or she may break through the earth on one side and step down to pull the child up—the sooner the better—and he or she need not get permission from a court of law, even though in the process of rescuing the child he or she may be building stairs.

And if a person sees a door shut on a room in which an infant is alone, he or she may break down the door to get the baby out—the sooner the better—and he or she need not get permission from a court of law, even though by breaking down the door he or she may knock off chips that can be used for firewood (Babylonian Talmud, *Yoma*, page 84b).

Piknah Nefesh or Not?

YES   NO   1. It is Yom Kippur, about 2:00 in the afternoon. Jon has been fasting. Jon is really hungry. He tells his friend, "I'm so hungry I could die," but he doesn't feel faint or anything. Can Jon eat?

YES   NO   2. It is Yom Kippur. Your little sister is a diabetic. You are concerned that her insulin level is out of balance and that her blood sugar level is dangerously low. She wants to continue the fast. You think she should eat. Should you insist that she eat?

YES   NO   3. It is the seventh night of Hanukkah. Cynthia's whole family is due at the JCC to see a Hanukkah play. The family lights the candles and then prepares to leave. Cynthia's mom wants to blow out the candles because she is worried that there might be an accident if they burned with no one around. Cynthia's brother says that it is against Jewish law to blow out Hanukkah candles. Should the family blow the Hanukkah candles out?

YES   NO   4. Larry does not keep kosher, but one day a bully in his school threatens to beat him up unless Larry eats a ham sandwich. The bully knows that Larry is Jewish and that Jews don't eat ham. Normally eating the sandwich wouldn't bother Larry. Should he eat it?

Pikuah Nefesh Experience

Work in small groups. Your grandfather decides that he wants to donate his body to science. He wants to donate his organs for transplant. Should you honor his wishes? Come up with a decision.

Pikuah Nefesh Resources

Transplants are the latest lifesaving frontier.

Gift of Life—Bone Marrow Donation
http://www.giftoflife.org/default.aspx

Gift Donor—Organ Donation
http://www.giftdonor.org/

Find where Judaism changed its view on organ transplantation.

רֵ֫לֶ֫ךְ VA·YELEKH

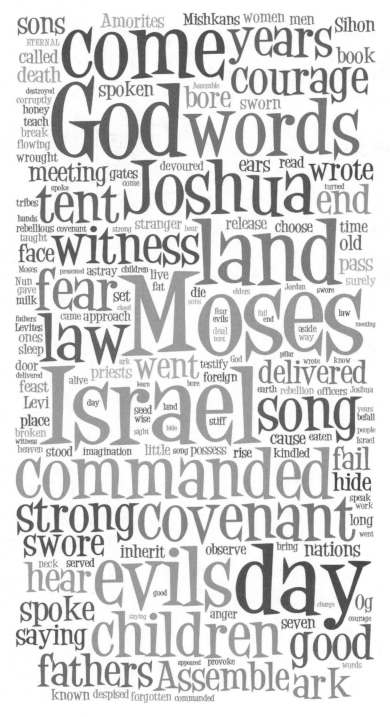

sons ETERNAL called death destroyed corruptly honey teach break flowing wrought Amorites Mishkans women men Sihon come years book courage spoken bore sworn Assemble God words destroyed spoke devoured ears read wrote meeting gates come Joshua turned end tribes tent hands rebellious covenant strong stranger hear release choose time old pass taught astray children live fat die elders Jordan swore surely face witness law Moses fail end aside way meeting Nun gave milk fathers Levites ones sleep fear set cloud came approach seed wise sight land hide stiff deal tent door delivered feast Levi alive priests went testify God bore foreign learn rebellion officers Joshua place broken witness heaven stood imagination little song possess rise kindled Israel song cause eaten years befall people Israel fail hide speak work long went commanded strong covenant swore inherit observe bring nations hear evils day Og neck served good saying anger charge courage spoke children seven good saying fathers Assemble ark known despised forgotten commanded appeared provoke words

Overview: Deuteronomy 31:1–31:30

Moses announces that Joshua will take over as his successor. He assures the people of Israel that God will still be with them. Moses gives Joshua public recognition that he has confidence in him as a leader. He then hands the law to the Levites to deposite in the *aron*.

OUR TORAH TEXT: DEUTERONOMY 31:19

Even though it is not obvious upon first reading, in this *sidrah* the Torah gives us one of the Torah mitzvot.

וְעַתָּה כִּתְבוּ לָכֶם אֶת־הַשִּׁירָה הַזֹּאת
וְלַמְּדָהּ אֶת־בְּנֵי־יִשְׂרָאֵל שִׂימָהּ בְּפִיהֶם
לְמַעַן תִּהְיֶה־לִּי הַשִּׁירָה הַזֹּאת לְעֵד בִּבְנֵי יִשְׂרָאֵל.

וְעַתָּה כִּתְבוּ לָכֶם אֶת הַשִּׁירָה הַזֹּאת
לַמְּדָהּ אֶת בְּנֵי יִשְׂרָאֵל שִׂימָהּ בְּפִיהֶם
לְמַעַן תִּהְיֶה לִּי הַשִּׁירָה הַזֹּאת לְעֵד
בִּבְנֵי יִשְׂרָאֵל

Now write down this song for yourself...

Exploring Our Torah Text

Writing a Torah

Every Jew is commanded to write a *sefer Torah* for his or her own use. Even if he or she has inherited a *sefer Torah*, it is a mitzvah to write one at his or her own expense. If he or she writes it with his or her own hand, it is as if he or she has received it at Mt. Sinai.

If he or she does not know how, he or she should have others write it. Anyone who corrects a single letter in a *sefer Torah* is credited with writing all of it (Rambam, *Mishneh Torah*, Laws of the *Sefer Torah*, 7:1).

The rabbis based the mitzvah that obligates every Jew to write a *sefer Torah* on this biblical verse:

וְעַתָּה כִּתְבוּ לָכֶם אֶת הַשִּׁירָה הַזֹּאת

THEREFORE, WRITE DOWN THIS SONG FOR YOURSELF
(Deuteronomy 31:19).

Even today a *sefer Torah* is handwritten by a *sofer* (scribe). Writing it is a long, hard process. It takes between nine months and a year of work to finish a Torah. It has to be written with the best permanent black ink, on parchment made from the skins of clean (kosher) animals. For a pen the *sofer* must use a quill or a reed. Metal, which is used to make weapons, cannot be used for making a Torah. All of the separate parchments must be sewn together with sinews from kosher animals, and the *sofer* must use a thorn for a needle.

The *sofer* cannot write a single letter from memory. The *sofer* must read from a correct text, pronounce every word out loud and only then copy it. Every letter and every word must be perfectly spaced. Every letter must be clearly drawn so that a child can recognize it. In addition, the *sofer* has to add crowns to thirteen letters. The letters צ, ץ, ג, י, ן, נ, ע, ש have three-stroke crowns, and the letters ה, י, ח, ק, ד, ב have one-stroke crowns.

Here is a passage handwritten by a *sofer*. Add the crowns on your own.

וְעַתָּה כַתְבוּ לָכֶם אֶת הַשִּׁירָה הַזֹּאת

To understand how hard it is to write a *sefer Torah*, look at this list of conditions that can make it un-kosher (and therefore unusable).
- If it was written on the skin of an unclean animal.
- If a clean skin was not made into parchment.
- If the parchment was not made specifically for a *sefer Torah*.
- If it was written on the wrong side of the parchment.
- If just one section was written on the wrong side of the parchment.

- If it was written without traced lines.
- If it was not written with indelible ink.
- If it was written in any language but Hebrew.
- If the sofer was a heretic or impure.
- If the sofer wrote the name of God without *kavanah* (devotion).
- If one letter was omitted.
- If one letter was added.
- If two letters touch.
- If one letter can be misread as another.
- If a letter can't be read.
- If one word looks like two.
- If two words look like one.
- If the *sofer* changed the form of any section.
- If it is not sewn together with the dry tendons of clean animals. (Rambam, *Mishneh Torah*, Laws of the *Sefer Torah*, 10:1)

torah experience

One Hasidic rabbi took the laws for writing a *sefer Torah* and explained them this way:

> The many letters in the Torah represent the many souls of the Jewish people. If one single letter is left out of the Torah, it is unfit for use. If one single soul is left out of the union of the Jewish people, the Divine Presence will not join them. Like the letters, the souls must join together in a union. Then why is it forbidden for one letter to touch another? Because every soul must have its own unique relationship with its Creator. (Rabbi Uri of Strelisk, from *Tales of the Hasidim: Later Masters*, Martin Buber, p. 147).

Reflection Question: Why does writing the Torah have so many rules?

MITZVAH OF THE WEEK: סֵפֶר תּוֹרָה WRITING A TORAH

It is a mitzvah for every Jew to write a Torah scroll for him/herself.

If one is unable to write a Torah scroll, he or she can fulfill this mitzvah by hiring a qualified *sofer* (scribe) who will write one for him or her. The *sofer* must be both skilled in this art and a religious Jew.

The writing of a *sefer Torah* must be done in accordance with certain rules and specifications.

- It must be written by hand.
- It must be written on sheets of parchment made from the skin of a kosher animal.
- It must be written with special Hebrew lettering.

Before beginning to write a *sefer Torah* the *sofer* must declare that the work is to be a *sefer Torah*.

The sheets of parchment that make up the Torah scroll must be sewn together with the tendons of a kosher animal.

The *sofer* must have before him/her a Torah scroll from which the *sofer* reads, pronouncing every word before inscribing it.

A *sefer Torah* that is beyond repair or is decayed must be buried in a Jewish cemetery.

Since a Torah scroll is the holiest religious article, it must be given the highest respect. Therefore, when someone passes by with a *sefer Torah* in hand, we must rise and remain standing and never turn our back to it.

Sefer Torah Experience

Be sure there is an actual Torah scroll open in the classroom to illustrate calligraphy to the students. Write mezuzah scrolls (even if just *Shema* and first line of *V'Ahavta*) or bring in a *sofer* as a guest.

YouTube has videos that show scribes writing Torah scrolls and giving Hebrew calligraphy demonstrations.

Reflection Question: How is a Torah like a person?

Sefer Torah Resources

The Torah uses music as a metaphor for Torah. Here are some music foundations (including Jewish Rock Radio).

 Jewish Rock Radio
http://jewishrockradio.com/

Fender Music Foundation
http://www.fendermusicfoundation.org/

 Save the Music Foundation
http://www.vh1savethemusic.com/

Young Musicians Foundation
http://www.ymf.org/

 Shalshelet Foundation
http://www.shalshelet.org/

Find some sites for Jewish music.

הַאֲזִינוּ HA-AZINU

Moses sings the Song of Moses, a farewell to the people. He reviews history and takes from it the lessons to be learned and taught. He urges the people to take these words to heart. The *parashah* concludes with God telling Moses that he is to ascend Mount Nebo and to see the Promised Land from afar, and there he will die.

OUR TORAH TEXT: DEUTERONOMY 32:52

The speeches are over. Moses begins to say his goodbyes. Our verse is pointing him toward his grave.

כִּי מִנֶּגֶד תִּרְאֶה אֶת־הָאָרֶץ וְשָׁמָּה לֹא תָבוֹא
אֶל־הָאָרֶץ אֲשֶׁר־אֲנִי נֹתֵן לִבְנֵי יִשְׂרָאֵל.

כי מנגד תראה את הארץ ושמה
לא תבוא אל הארץ אשר אני נתן
לבני ישראל

For you shall not see the land that is still far off. You shall not go to the Land that I give to the Families-of-Israel.

Exploring Our Torah Text

This Torah Portion is Moses' ethical will.

What is an ethical will? It is a letter a parent writes to his or her children. In it, a mother describes what she has learned during her life and the lessons she hopes to pass on to her children and future generations. The blessings Moses gives the Jewish people in this *parashah* are like an ethical will. Some ethical wills are lengthy, containing many details, while others are only several sentences in length. An ethical will becomes part of a family's inheritance and heritage. It is considered by some to be much more important than the passing on of material possessions.

An ethical will can preserve a memory and, to some extent, shape the way that a person is remembered. That is one of the greatest challenges and the greatest dangers in writing an ethical will. We all wish we had done more in our lives. We

259

have to fight the desire to be remembered for things that we wish we had done but never got around to doing. Here is an examples of an ethical will. As you read them, ask yourself what they tell you about the authors.

The RAMBAN (Rabbi Moshe ben Na<u>h</u>man), a great scholar who lived in the thirteenth century in Spain, wrote the following to his children and students:

> Listen, my child, to the instruction of your father, and do not forget the teaching of your mother (Proverbs 1:8). Speak with kindness to all people always. This will save you from anger, the major cause of misdeed...Always be humble; regard every person as greater than yourself...Study Torah regularly so that you can fulfill its commandments. When you finish your studies, think carefully about what you have learned; try to translate your learning into action... When you pray, do not think about worldly matters, think only of God...Read this letter once a week, and be regular in carrying out its requirements. By doing so you will always walk in the path of God, and you will be worthy of all of the good that is due to the righteous.

Underline the values that the Ramban wants to pass on to his children.

Why does he ask that the letter be read every week?

> IMAGINE...You are going to be a parent. Not years from now, but in the next few days! To say the least, it will be quite an adjustment. Before the birth of your child, close your eyes, take a deep breath and think for a moment about having a child. What are your hopes and dreams for your child? What kind of person do you hope he or she will be? What kind of Jew?

Use the space below to write your thoughts down in the form of a letter to your unborn child that you will present when he or she is ready to start a family.

_____

_____

_____

_____

_____

_____

_____

_____

_____

_____

eXPerieNCiNG tHe toraH

Go to YouTube to search for and watch ethical wills. Then tape one of your own and send it to your parents.

Reflection Question: Do you think you can influence the future?

MITZVAH OF THE WEEK: OBEYING A LAST WILL AND TESTAMENT

It is a mitzvah to carry out the wishes of a person who has died. Thus it is a duty of the legal heirs to carry out the wishes of a person who wrote a will, and this is a duty the courts will enforce. However, the above rule is not always to be applied as a strict legal duty, and when the duty is merely a moral one, the court will not compel compliance with the wishes of the person who wrote the will's directions (*Shevut Ya'akov*, vol. 1, no. 168).

Mitzvah Experience

A living will or an advanced directive is an end-of-life document. It helps your relatives by telling them what you want to happen medically and by telling them what you don't want to happen to you.

Download and fill out one of these forms at
http://www.caringinfo.org

Part II

Bring a copy of the forms home. Have your parents fill them out. It is nothing that you will need now. But when you are an adult and your parents are old, it will save asking a lot of questions you don't want to ask.

וְזֹאת הַבְּרָכָה
V'ZOT HA-BRAKHAH

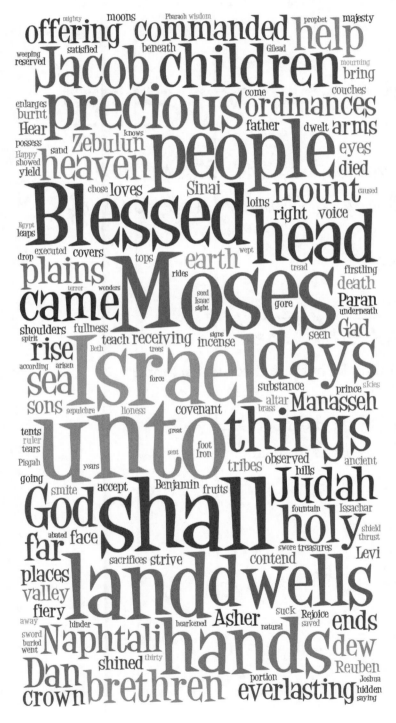

Overview:
Deuteronomy
33:1–34:12

Moses blesses the Families-of-Israel tribe by tribe. Moses goes up to Mt. Nebo, has a chance to see the Promised Land one more time and dies. The people mourn him for thirty days. The Torah concludes with the verse "And there never again was a prophet in Israel like Moses, who knew God face to face" (Deut. 34:10).

263

OUR TORAH TEXT: DEUTERONOMY 34:5

This is the end of the Torah. Not quite the last verse, but close to it. This is the moment when Moses dies.

וַיָּמָת שָׁם מֹשֶׁה עֶבֶד־יי בְּאֶרֶץ מוֹאָב
עַל־פִּי יי.

וימת שם משה עבד י בארץ מואב
על פי יי

Moses, the servant of the Eternal, died there in the land of Moav, by the mouth of God.

Exploring Our Torah Text

What do you make of these three translations?

JPS: by the word of God.

Literal: by the mouth of God.

Rashi: by a kiss from God.

torah experience

This script comes from *Midrash P'tirat Moshe*, a collection of rabbinic fantasies about the way Moses died. It is not supposed to be a collection of facts about his death; rather, it is a way of talking about deeper truths. Our version is drawn from the edition found in *Sefer ha-Aggadah*.

Prologue

Narrator: AND THE ETERNAL SAID TO MOSES:

God: BEHOLD, IT IS GETTING CLOSE TO YOUR DAYS TO DIE (Deuteronomy 31.14).

Narrator: Even Moses had to die. It says in the book of Job:

Bible: EVEN IF HE GOES UP TO HEAVEN, AND HIS HEAD REACHES UP TO THE CLOUDS, STILL HE SHALL DIE (Job 20:6).

Narrator: This is the story of Moses, who went up to heaven, walked on clouds like an angel, spoke to God face to face and received the Torah from God's hand. Yet as soon as he reached the time for the natural end to his life, God told him:

God: BEHOLD, IT IS GETTING CLOSE TO YOUR DAYS TO DIE (Deuteronomy 31.14).

Scene 1: "I'll Fluff, And I'll Puff And I'll Pray Your Gates Down."

Narrator: When Moses realized that God's decree about his death had been sealed, he drew a circle in the dirt, stood inside it and shouted:

Moses: Master-of-the-Universe, I will not move out of this circle until You change Your mind and take back the decree.

Narrator: He put on sackcloth and ashes and stood praying and petitioning God. Soon heaven, earth and all of creation were shaking. Everyone was afraid that God was going to destroy the world and start again.

God: Close the gates of heaven. Do not let Moses' prayers and requests enter. I do not want to hear them.

Narrator: But Moses' cries began to cut through the heavenly gates like a blowtorch. God ordered the ministering angels:

God: Bolt every gate in heaven!

Moses: Master-of-the-Universe! You know all the pain and suffering I endured until the Families of Israel believed in You. You know how hard it was to teach them Torah and the mitzvot. All I want is to see a little of their happiness after all those years of pain in the wilderness. Is that too much to ask? Yet now You tell me, "You shall not pass over the Jordan." Oh, God! In that case Your Torah is a lie—it is unjust—because Your own law says: "An employer is commanded to pay his hired servant on the day he finishes work" (Leviticus 19:13). So how come I had to work for forty years to try to get Israel to be a holy and faithful nation, and I get nothing?

God: This is still my decree!

Scene 2 Moses Plays "Let's Make A Deal"

Moses: If You won't let me enter the Promised Land alive, then how about letting me be brought in dead, like Joseph's bones?

God: Moses, when Joseph went down to Egypt he did not hide the fact that he was a Hebrew. He told everyone about his Jewish identity. However, when you arrived in Midian you let people think you were an Egyptian.

Moses: Well, if You won't bring me into the Land, then at least let me be like one of the beasts of the field that eats grass, drinks the stream waters and looks out at the world.

God: Stop! Enough! No!

Moses: Then let me fly like a bird that goes searching in all directions for its food and then comes back to its nest at day's end.

God: Enough already! Stop! No more!

Scene 3: A Friend In Need...

Narrator: Next Moses turned to the heavens and the earth.

Moses: Intercede for me. Help me to change God's mind.

Heavens & Earth: We have ourselves to worry about. Our time is limited, too. We've been warned. Remember?

Bible: The heavens shall disappear like smoke, and the earth shall wear out like old clothes (Isaiah 51:6).

Narrator: Then Moses asked the sun, moon and stars to help.

Moses: Pray for me!

Sun, Moon, Stars:	We've got our own worries. We will die, too. We've been warned, too. Listen:
Bible:	ALL OF THE OBJECTS OF HEAVEN SHALL BE DISSOLVED (Isaiah 34:4).
Narrator:	Moses went to the mountains and hills.
Moses:	Pray for me!
Mountains & Hills:	We can't help you—we first have to beg for ourselves. We've got to save ourselves. We've been warned as well:
Bible:	FOR THE MOUNTAINS WILL DEPART, AND THE HILLS WILL BE REMOVED (Isaiah 54:10).
Narrator:	Next on Moses' list was the sea.
Moses:	Pray for mercy for me.
The Sea:	Son of Amram, what makes today different than yesterday? Aren't you the same son of Amram who beat me with his staff and divided me into twelve tiny streams? I had no way of defending myself against you, because you stood at God's right hand. I had nowhere I could go for help. Now the tables are turned; you come and ask me to help you. Why should I help you?
Moses:	Would that I were back in the old days. I used to stand by the Reed Sea as if I were a king—but now I cry for help, and no one listens to me.
Narrator:	Next Moses sneaked into heaven and cornered one of the ministering angels.
Moses:	I beg of you—please pray for mercy for me.
Angel:	Moses, my teacher, why are you going to all this bother? It can't do any good. I already know from the Inner Court that your prayers will not be heard on this matter.

Scene 4: Solo, The Face-To-Face

Narrator:	Moses places his hands on his head and starts to cry.
Moses:	To whom can I go? Who will intercede with God to have mercy on me?
Narrator:	God was getting angrier and angrier with Moses. The more he begged, the angrier God got. That is until Moses prayed with the words:

Moses: THE ETERNAL, THE ETERNAL THE GOD, THE MERCIFUL, THE GRACIOUS (Exodus 34:6).

Narrator: Right away God's anger subsided. God again spoke to Moses:

God: Moses, do you remember that I took two oaths? The first was to destroy Israel after they had worshiped the Golden Calf. The second was that you would die and not enter the Promised Land. I gave up and cancelled the first oath when you prayed. Now you want Me to forget My second oath. You are holding onto both ends of the rope; it doesn't work that way. If you want Me to answer this prayer, then I will restore the first oath and destroy Israel. Otherwise, if you want that oath to remain in effect, you must withdraw your present prayer.

Moses: Master-of-the-Universe, better Moses and a thousand like him have to die before a single fingernail on one Israelite be hurt.

Master-of-the-Universe! Are You really going to let the feet that came up on high and the face that looked face-to-face with God and the hands that received the Torah directly from You sleep in the dirt?

God: That is My plan, and that is the law of life. Each generation will have its own teachers and its own leaders. Until now you've been the one to serve Me. From now on that will be Joshua your servant's responsibility.

Moses: Master-of-the-Universe, I have to die because it's Joshua's turn to become the leader. Why not just let me be his disciple?

God: If that is what you want to do, go and do it.

Scene 5: Moses, The Servant Of Joshua

Narrator: So Moses got up early in the morning and went to the door of Joshua's tent. Joshua was seated, busy teaching Torah. Moses quietly entered with his hand on his heart. Joshua was focused on his teaching and didn't notice Moses. Meanwhile, many Israelites had gone to Moses' tent door, wanting to study Torah with him. They asked:

Israelites: Where is Moses our teacher?

Narrator: They were told that he had gone to Joshua's tent. They followed and found him standing there while Joshua sat and taught Torah.

Israelites: Joshua! What is the meaning of this? How can you sit and teach while Moses is standing?

Narrator: Joshua raised his eyes and saw Moses standing. He cried:

Joshua: Rabbi, Rabbi, Father, Father!

Israelites: Moses, teach us Torah.

Moses: I am not permitted.

Israelites: We will not abandon you!

Moses: From now on you must learn Torah from Joshua.

Narrator: They accepted this command and sat down to hear the teachings of Joshua. Joshua sat at the head, Moses at his right hand and the sons of Aaron at his left. Joshua taught Torah in the presence of Moses, his teacher. This is the way the mantle of authority and wisdom passed from Moses to Joshua.

Later Moses and Joshua went to the *Mishkan*. There the cloud of the *Shekhinah* came down and divided them. Then it was gone.

Moses: What did God have to say?

Joshua: I am not allowed to tell you, just as you were not permitted to tell me everything when God used to speak to you.

Moses: Better one thousand deaths than a single jealousy! Oh Master-of-the-Universe, up to now I sought life, but now I am ready to return my soul to You!

Scene 6: Meanwhile, Back In Heaven...

God: WHO WILL NOW RISE UP FOR ME AGAINST EVIL DOERS? (Psalm 94:16). Who will now defend Israel against My anger? Who will stand by to pray for them when they are at war? Who will seek My mercy when they sin against Me?

Narrator: The first to speak was Metatron, God's personal ministering angel and Israel's number-one advocate. Metatron was the angel who kept the book of Israel's good deeds.

Metatron: Master-of-the-Universe! Moses is now dying in accordance with Your law. Why then do You mourn?

God: Let me tell you a story: Once there was a king of flesh and blood who had a son who angered him by his wild and rebellious behavior. In fact, the king often got so angry that he wanted to kill the son but was prevented from doing so by the queen, who saved her son. Then the queen died, and the king deeply mourned her. When his ministers asked the reason for the depth of his sadness, he answered, "I am not only mourning for my wife, but also for my son. Many times I have been so angry with him that I would have killed him, if not for his mother. His mother saved him every time."

This is exactly how I feel. I am mourning not only for Moses but for Israel, because every time they angered Me, Moses stood by them, defended them and took away My anger.

Narrator: God then spoke to Gabriel, the angel who guards paradise and will eventually blow the great shofar:

God: Go and bring home the soul of Moses.

Gabriel: Master-of-the-Universe, how can I be witness to the death of one who is the equal of the six hundred thousand Israelites?

Narrator: So then God turned to Michael, another one of the four angels in God's inner circle. He was the commando angel who always defended Israel. He was the angel who taught Moses Torah.

God: Go and bring home the soul of Moses.

Michael: I was his teacher, and he was my pupil. How can I bring about his death?

Narrator: Finally God turned to Sammael, the chief of the angels who worked for Satan, the prosecuting angel. He was the angel of death. Now Sammael had been waiting hourly for Moses' death and had been asking:

Sammael: When will the moment come when I will be able to take away his soul? When will I get to see Michael weep as my mouth fills with joy?

God: Go and bring home the soul of Moses.

Narrator: When God finally gave him the command, he clothed himself in anger, put on his sword, wrapped himself in his cloak of terror and went out to Moses.

Scene 7: Moses vs. Sammael

Narrator: When Sammael came to Moses, Moses was busy writing God's name in a *sefer Torah*. Moses glowed with light. He was as bright as the sun. He looked a lot like an angel. Sammael was afraid. He was terrified. He couldn't speak.

Moses: Wicked one, what are you doing here?

Sammael: I have come to take away your soul.

Moses: Who sent you?

Sammael: The One-Who-Created-All-Things.

Moses: Get away from here. I wish to praise the Holy-One-Who-Is-to-Be-Praised: "I SHALL NOT DIE BUT LIVE IF I TELL OF GOD'S WORKS" (Psalm 118:17).

Sammael: Don't be so high and mighty. God already has someone to sing praises: "THE HEAVENS DECLARE THE GLORY OF GOD" (Psalm 19:2).

Moses: I can shut them up. "HEAVENS, LISTEN AND I WILL SPEAK. LET THE EARTH HEAR THE WORDS OF MY MOUTH" (Deuteronomy 32:1).

Sammael: But all living things must return their souls to me!

Moses: Yes, but I have more power than any other living thing.

Sammael: What is your power?

Moses: I am the son of Amram, who at the age of three prophesied that I would receive the Torah in the midst of flames. I went into a king's place and removed the crown from the king's head. When I was eighty I performed signs and miracles in Egypt and brought out six hundred thousand Jews despite the might of Egypt. I divided the sea; I climbed up and made a way to heaven. I fought a battle with the angels who didn't want me to receive the Torah. I spoke to God face to face and received the Torah from God's right hand and taught it to Israel. 1 also caused the sun and the moon to stand still in heaven. Who else in all the world has done such things? Go away. I will not give my soul to you.

Narrator: Sammael went back to God and told him what had happened.

God: Go back and bring the soul of Moses back here.

Narrator: Sammael unsheathed his sword and stood at Moses' side. Moses became angry with him. He took his staff with God's

271

name inscribed on it. He hit Sammael with all his might, and the angel fled. Moses continued to chase him away. Then Moses took a beam of light from between his eyes and blinded the angel of death.

Scene 8: God Steps In

God: Moses, the hour has come. You must now depart from the world.

Moses: Master-of-the-Universe. Remember when You appeared to me from the burning bush. Do you remember how I stood on Mt. Sinai for forty days and forty nights? I beg You, do not deliver me into the hands of the angel of death.

God: Fear not, Moses. I Myself will attend to you and bury you.

Moses: All right, but please give me a couple of moments. I want to bless Israel. All these years they have only gotten orders, warnings and scoldings from me.

Narrator: So Moses began to bless each tribe separately. When he saw that the hour was drawing to a close he united the tribes for a single blessing.

Moses: I have troubled you much with the Torah and the mitzvot. Now forgive me.

Israelites: Moses, our teacher and our leader, you are forgiven.

Narrator: Then the people drew close to him.

Israelites: We have frequently made you very angry and given you much distress. Forgive us!

Moses: You are forgiven.

God: The moment has arrived for you to depart from this world.

Moses: Bless the Name of The One Who lives and exists forever.

Narrator: He then turned back to the Israelites and said:

Moses: Please, when you enter the Land, remember me and my bones and say, "Alas for the son of Amram, who ran bravely before us but whose bones fell in the wilderness."

God: Now you must depart from the world.

Moses: Now you see the destiny of all living things.

Narrator: Moses sanctified himself like the angels. Then God descended with his four closest ministering angels from the highest heaven to retrieve the soul of Moses. The angels stood around Moses.

God: Moses, close your eyes. Now place your hands on your breast. Bring your feet together. Precious soul, I set a time of one hundred and twenty years for you to be in the body of Moses. Now the time has come for you to depart. Please leave the body—do not wait.

Moses' Soul: Master-of-the-Universe. I know that You are the God of all spirits and the Master of all souls. You created me and placed me in the body of Moses for one hundred and twenty years. Now I ask, is there a better body in the entire world than that of Moses? I love him, and I don't want to leave him.

God: Come with Me, and I will raise you to the highest heaven and set you down beneath the throne of my glory—right alongside the cherubim and seraphim.

Narrator: At that moment God kissed Moses and removed his soul with a kiss. Then God wept:

God: THERE HAS NEVER ARISEN IN ISRAEL SINCE THEN ANOTHER PROPHET WHO CAN BE COMPARED TO MOSES (Deuteronomy 34:10).

Narrator: And the heavens wept:

Heavens: THE GODLY MAN IS PERISHED FROM THE EARTH (Micah 7:2).

Narrator: The earth wept:

Earth: AND THE MOST UPRIGHT AMONG MEN IS NO MORE (Micah 7:2).

Narrator: The ministering angels wept:

Angels: HE DID THE ETERNAL'S JUSTICE (Deuteronomy 33:21).

Narrator: Israel wept:

Israelites: HE BROUGHT THE ETERNAL'S JUDGMENT TO ISRAEL (Deuteronomy 33:21).

All: HE ENTERS INTO PEACE. EVERY ONE THAT WALKS IN RIGHTEOUSNESS RESTS PEACEFULLY (Isaiah 57:2).

MITZVAH OF THE WEEK: כְּתְבוּ לָכֶם תּוֹרָה WRITE YOURSELF A TORAH

Write this song for yourself (*Deuteronomy* 31.19).

This is the last mitzvah in the Torah. Every Jew is supposed to write his or her own Torah. If you don't have the skills, then you can pay someone to do it for you.

When you write a *sefer Torah*:

- you must write it by hand.
- you must write it on sheets of parchment.
- you must write it in Hebrew.
- you must start with a meditation.
- you must sew the sheet together with sinews of clean animals.
- you must copy it from a kosher sefer Torah.
- you must pronounce every word before you write it.

K'tuv Lekhem Et Ha-Shirah Ha-Zot Experience

There are stories about Jews in the former Soviet Union (FSU) who recreated books and history from memory. They would ask every visitor to fill in a piece. Work as a committee without any resources and write down as much of the Torah as you can from memory.

Reflection Question: Why does the Torah want every Jew to write his or her own copy of the Torah?